Easy
HOME
Organizer

Easy HOME *Organizer*

15-Minute Step-by-Step Solutions

VICKI PAYNE

Sterling Publishing Services.
New York

Prolific Impressions Production Staff:

Editor in Chief: Mickey Baskett
Copy Editor: Phyllis Mueller
Graphics: Dianne Miller, Karen Turpin
Styling: Lenos Key
Photography: Jerry Mucklow
Administration: Jim Baskett

Library of Congress Cataloging-in-Publication Data
Payne, Vicki.
  Easy home organizer : 15-minute step-by-step solutions / Vicki Payne.
      p. cm.
  Includes index.
  ISBN-13: 978-1-4027-2442-8   3688 8468 12/07
  ISBN-10: 1-4027-2442-X
1. Home economics. 2. Time management. 3. Storage in the home. 4. Organization. I. Title.
TX147.P296 2007
640--dc22
                                                                                          2006027139

2   4   6   8   10 9   7   5   3   1

Published by Sterling Publishing Co., Inc.
387 Park Avenue South, New York, NY 10016
© 2007 by Prolific Impressions, Inc.
Distributed in Canada by Sterling Publishing
c/o Canadian Manda Group, 165 Dufferin Street,
Toronto, Ontario, Canada M6K 3H6
Distributed in the United Kingdom by GMC Distribution Services,
Castle Place, 166 High Street, Lewes, East Sussex, England BN7 1XU
Distributed in Australia by Capricorn Link (Australia) Pty. Ltd.
P.O. Box 704, Windsor, NSW 2756, Australia

Printed in China
All rights reserved

ISBN-13: 978-1-4027-2442-8
ISBN-10: 1-4027-2442-X

For information about custom editions, special sales, premium and
corporate purchases, please contact Sterling Special Sales
Department at 800-805-5489 or specialsales@sterlingpub.com.

ABOUT
THE AUTHOR
VICKI PAYNE

Vicki Payne is an internationally recognized craft and home improvement expert and host of two national television series *For Your Home* and *Glass with Vicki Payne.* She has established herself as one of the craft industry's most successful and respected entrepreneurs. As CEO of Cutters Productions, she has produced 1,000s of how-to videos with more than 17 years of quality television programming-including 5 national weekly series and dozens of successful fund raisers for public television. Cutters has been awarded "Best Performing Pledge Specials" awards in 2003 and 2004 and the 2005 MVP award from American Public Television.

Cutters series and specials are carried by more than 284 public television stations, the Create Channel and AmericanLifeTV on cable throughout the United States. A few of the popular shows are: *For Your Home, Paint, Paper and Crafts, Glass with Vicki Payne, Kid Concoctions* and the *Donna Dewberry Show.* Vicki is a frequent and popular guest on a number of HGTV and The Discovery Channel programs as well as home improvement and crafting shows. She hosted the DIY Crafting series and along with her daughter, Sloan they host the *Handmade Gifts* workshops on the DIY Network.

In addition to her work in television, Vicki is an accomplished writer, speaker, and educator. She is frequently published in shelter, craft and trade magazines. She has authored and published many glass crafting books. Vicki is the author of *Stained Glass in an Afternoon* (Sterling, 2002), *Traditional Leaded Glass Crafting* (Sterling, 2003), and *The Stained Glass Classroom* (Sterling, 2004). She is an executive board member of the Art Glass Association and a member of the Craft and Hobby Association and Women In the Home Furnishing Industry.

ACKNOWLEDGEMENTS

Thank you to the following companies for their help in providing product and photos for this book.

EK Success

Riverside Furniture Company

Art Bin

KitchenShelves.Com

Space Savers

Joyce Leland and Sloan Payne-Rutter

Contents

How many times have you told yourself, "I've got to get this place organized! My closets, my drawers, my rooms – they are out of control!" But the task is so overwhelming that you end up doing nothing, continue complaining about the chaos, and beat yourself up for not being better organized.

Take heart! This book will help you change this lifetime pattern, and you'll have some fun and achieve daily bliss in the process. It's the little things in our everyday lives that make us crazy, like "Where are the car keys?" or "I can't find my shoes," or "Why are the kids' backpacks cluttering up the entry hall?" Sound familiar? This book is about the little things, things you can do in as little as 15 minutes or as much as a couple of hours that will make your everyday life less stressful and less messy.

Then there's attitude adjustment. Once everything has a home, you will need to train your family members to bring items home (put them away) after they use them. This may be harder than finding everything a home, but you can't have an organized home without both – a home for everything and the right attitude.

Make a list of simple little organization projects that would improve your day. And ask each family member to make a list, too. Then sit down together and compare your lists. If your family is like mine, you will find lots of similarities. Just like you, your kids are frustrated when they can't find things like soccer shoes or a favorite shirt on the day of the class picture.

This book contains ideas for solving the problems you have

Convenient, Creative, and Do-able Solutions for Creating Calm Out of Chaos

Start with yourself. What is it that makes you a little crazy every day? Every morning when you start your day are you met with disorganization? Maybe it is your make-up drawer, filled with unused lipsticks and two pink blushers you will never wear, that clutters up your morning, day after day.

Take a look around you as you sit reading this book. What do you see? Does everything have a home or do you see chaos? The concept of "home," was coined by professional organizers. It means that each and every item has a place, a home. A home for bills could be a basket or a wall-hanging organizer. For sporting equipment, home could be a plastic tub in the garage or a specially designed storage unit that hangs on the wall. If everything has a "home," it is easy to keep your home neat and organized.

identified on your list. Determine which area of your home is most problematic, turn to that section, and get to work.

Begin every organizing project by reducing the amount of stuff you have. In large part, we are disorganized because of the things that we keep and never use. They take up space, make us feel guilty, and add stress to our holidays. We all need to simplify our lives by adopting a philosophy of "less is best." Why store items you don't need or use? If you have clothes you don't wear (and who doesn't?), get rid of them. If you have toys no one plays with anymore, donate them to a children's center, hospital, or charity. Letting go of the things you don't need or use is the first step to organizing your home and your life.

Let's get started!

When we finally got a place of our own, I had a vision of what it would be like to live there. In my dream, I saw lots of parties and great evenings and afternoons spent sharing my life with my friends and family. What's your vision, your dream?

Every person's needs are different. Every family is different. Some of us have larger families, more hobbies, bigger collections, and just lots more junk! So it's important to assess your own family's needs and decide what will work best for all concerned.

Remember that the best way to get the full cooperation of all family members is to ask for their input, then have them help set the rules and participate in keeping the house organized. If you want to raise an organized child you have to set a good example and teach them how at an early age. They will thank you for it later, and you'll enjoy a well-organized home without stressing out.

Vicki Payne

Get rid of what you don't use.

———

Be honest about what you need.

———

Be ruthless about eliminating

the excess.

———

Don't buy more than you can store.

———

Have a home for everything.

If everything has a "home," it is easy to keep your home neat and organized

CHAPTER 1

Clutter Containment

Keeping an organized house is not a one-person job, even if you live alone. You need help – in the form of baskets, jars, plastic containers, and the good old cardboard box. In this first chapter, I'll show you some of my favorites and list some guidelines for choosing the right container for the job.

CONTAINER SHOPPING

- Measure your space and the items that you need to store before shopping so you'll know what size containers you need.
- Buy a variety of containers – more than you think you'll use. Chances are, once you get into organizing, you'll need more containers than you initially thought you would.
- Save the receipts. You can always return the ones you don't use.

Pictured opposite page: Shelves hold audio and video equipment. A variety of containers, including natural willow baskets, a triple wooden file box, and a clear plastic rack keep CDs, DVDs, videotapes, and remote controls organized and easy to use.

WOVEN WONDERS

"Woven wonders" – that's what I call baskets. There aren't many storage problems the right basket can't solve. No icon of style is older than the basket; archaeologists discovered baskets were used in the American Southwest as far back as 6000 B.C. Homemakers throughout the ages have relied on woven wonders to solve their housekeeping problems.

With their rich textures and warm tones, baskets are at home all over the house, organizing living rooms, bedrooms, kitchens, and bathrooms. From hiding stereo speakers to organizing laundry, baskets are our best clutter containers.

Types of Baskets

Baskets take many shapes and forms. They can be round or square or rectangular or oval, tall or short, deep or shallow, wide or narrow. They might have lids or handles. Most are made of natural materials like rattan, willow, wood, wicker, or grapevine, but they can also be made of other materials, such as wire.

The highest quality baskets are rattan baskets, which are hand crafted with rattan peel over sturdy rattan-core frames. Although expensive, they dress up any environment.

Pictured above: A wall-hung basket keeps clean rolled-up hand towels within easy reach and becomes part of the bathroom's décor.

Benefits & Considerations

Square or Rectangular Baskets
Benefit:
• Easy to line up on open shelves.
Consideration:
• Sizes are not standard – you may have to search several stores to find the right ones for your space.

Baskets with Handles
Benefit:
• Easy to carry from room to room.
Consideration:
• Handles may not support heavy loads.

What can be stored in a basket?

Laundry
Clothes
Bed linens
Rolled towels
Magazines
Vegetables
Flatware
Office supplies
Mail
Toys
Keys
Pet leashes
Hats, gloves, scarves
Stereo speakers
Remote controls

Woven Trays
Benefits:
• Wonderful for displaying items on an ottoman or coffee table.
• Excellent for serving beverages and food indoors or out.
• Great for holding small objects on counters and dresser tops.
Considerations:
• If the bottom is irregular, items can tip over and spill.
• Must be sturdy to transport items from kitchen to table.

Pictured left: Bin-type baskets on a shelf store remote controls and DVDS. Bin baskets and angled baskets (the type where the front of the basket is shorter than the back) are great for storing items on shelves that are close together because the contents are visible. Use them for items you don't want to keep out of sight.

Round Baskets

Benefits:
- Hat box styles look great in bedrooms and bathrooms, especially if they have lids and can be stacked.
- Rolled towels and magazines fit nicely in round baskets.
- Available in a large variety of widths and heights.

Considerations:
- Round baskets take up more space on shelves.
- If used to store square or rectangular items (papers, books, DVDs), you'll have lots of unused space.

Hampers

Benefits:
- Available in a wide variety of sizes shapes and colors.
- Blend easily with any decor.
- Can be placed in highly visible locations without looking utilitarian.

Considerations:
- If not lined, a wicker hamper can snag delicate or loosely woven fabrics.
- Without a hinged lid, they are difficult to open when your arms are full of dirty laundry.
- Basket hampers are more expensive than plastic ones.
- For moisture and mildew resistance, look for wicker hampers coated with PVC.

Baskets with Lids

Benefits:
- Keep contents cleaner and less dusty than open baskets.
- Can be stacked.
- Conceal contents so things look neat and tidy.

Considerations:
- Contents must be a good fit or the lid won't close.
- Can't see what's inside without removing the lid.
- Limited sizes, colors, and styles available.

CLEAR AS GLASS

Glass containers are great for storage and display. They come in a variety of shapes and sizes. Contents stay dry and are easily accessible, and (best of all) you can see what you have stored. While glass provides many benefits, its disadvantage is that it can break if dropped or treated roughly.

There are three important considerations when selecting

Buy containers that have multiple uses.

glass containers. First is the location (where will you be using or storing the container). For example, glass containers are great in the bathroom if the bathroom is not used by children or clumsy adults. (Then plastic containers are a better choice.) The second consideration is the contents (what will you be storing) – do you want the contents to be in view?

The third is the size and shape of the container. Buy containers that have multiple uses. This season you might use one to store cotton balls, next season it might be sponges. When selecting a glass container, look for one with a wide mouth (opening) so a variety of objects can easily fit inside and just as easily be retrieved. Glass canisters are perfect – they are made from thicker glass so they don't chip or break as easily as thinner ones. If you are looking for a container to store items like sea shells, take the largest shell you have to the store with you. That way, you'll know the size is right.

Labels for Jars

Depending on the color of the glass or the items you are storing in the container, you may want to label them. A label is especially handy on jars you use in the pantry or garage to store everyday items. With a label, you can quickly see what was used up and add that item to your shopping list. Labels also help with quick cleanup and pickup if everyone can clearly identify where certain items go.

For labeling, I like to use a permanent black marker that's designed for writing on glass. It stays on the surface until you use a little soap and water to remove it. You can also tie decorative card tags around the necks of jars with string or ribbon for a creative, stylish look. Other options are labels created with a label maker or paper secured with clear tape.

Recycled Jars

Recycled food jars are free – once you've eaten the food, the jars are a bonus. They are usually very durable and generally have lids that seal. Wide-mouth jars (canning jars, pickle jars, baby food jars) are some of my favorites. (A small opening on a large jar makes it difficult to store large items.)

Baby food jars are so great for holding small items like nails, screws, pins, flower seeds, and spices. Or use them in your home office to hold paper clips, rubber bands, pushpins and thumbtacks, or staples as well as pencils and pens.

Most food jars have metal lids. For a coordinated look, paint them. Place the metal lids on some newspaper and give them a couple coats of spray paint. Choose a color that matches your decor or coordinates with other storage containers. You could also devise a system of color-coordinated lids to denote the items you are storing in them. For example, use blue lids for jars of screws, yellow for nuts and bolts, and green for nails and tacks.

Benefits & Considerations

Bowls
Benefits:
- Come in a variety of shapes, sizes, and colors
- You can see what's inside

Considerations:
- Best for storing lightweight items made of wood, paper, and plastic, as opposed to metal items like keys.

Recycled Jars with Lids (such as peanut butter jars)
Benefits:
- Wide mouth for easy access.
- Lids keep contents clean and dry.

Considerations:
- Larger sizes can be heavy.
- Difficult to find in a variety of affordable sizes.

Vases
Benefits:
- Great storage containers for pens, markers, and other art supplies.
- Look stylish on desks and shelves.

Consideration:
- Glass is thin and breaks easily

Wine Bottles
Benefits:
- Can be fitted with pouring spouts for dish soap, olive oil, or condiments.
- Available in interesting shapes and colors.

Consideration:
- Small opening limits their use – best for liquids.

Large wide-mouth jars like this glass canister are perfect for storing groups of items. Here a collection of seashells has a storage home with a tag that labels when the shells were collected. Because the collection is so pretty, it can be a decorative accessory as well.

CARDBOARD BOXES

The most affordable and easily obtainable storage containers are boxes made of corrugated cardboard or papier mache. Cardboard can be recycled for free from lots of sources or bought at office supply, moving supply, or container stores. Boxes come in a wide variety of shapes and sizes and are lightweight. They are not, however, impervious to moisture, dust, and bugs, and most of them are not attractive. (Having stacks of them around the house suggests you're moving out instead of getting organized.) And once something goes into a cardboard box, unless you are moving, the box may become its final home. (What we can't see, we don't remember; therefore, we don't use.)

Having said that, there are some items I do store in cardboard boxes. Papier mache containers such as file boxes and cardboard magazine holders are great for office storage. Photo boxes are great for photos, letters, and cards I want to keep and access easily. I also like cardboard boxes for storing vintage clothes and linens because they allow the fabric to breathe. Tip: For storing textiles, buy acid-free boxes, and label them for easy identification.

Benefits & Considerations

Underbed Storage Boxes

Benefits:

- Allow you to gain extra storage under the bed or on upper closet shelves.
- A variety of colors and designs available. Tip: Seasonal designs make it easy to tell what is stored inside.

Consideration:

- Lids don't fit tightly and can become bent or flattened.

Papier Mache Boxes

Benefit:

- Easy to decorate with paper, fabric, paint, and rubber stamps.
- Very affordable.

Consideration:

- Heavy loads and age can cause corners to split and come apart.

Boxes for Holiday Storage

Our boxes are sometimes as important as what we store inside them. I love using cardboard boxes for Christmas decorations – they are a tradition at my house. When my children and husband see those old familiar boxes they really get into the Christmas spirit. One of my favorites is the box my son's toy train set came in 30 years ago. It serves as the storage container for vintage ornaments, but its real purpose is to give us an excuse to reminisce about Christmases past.

Cardboard boxes also provide strong support for items such outdoor lights and glass decorations. As your collection grows, you can easily increase the size of the box. You can find boxes designed specifically for larger items (wreaths, artificial trees) at better container stores. Since these items tend to be somewhat expensive, it's worth spending some money to store them properly.

project

HOW TO COVER A CARDBOARD BOX

Give ordinary cardboard magazine holders from the office supply or discount store a custom look with fabric and upholstery braid.

YOU'LL NEED:

Cardboard magazine holder, fabric of your choice, upholstery braid in a coordinating color, spring-type clothespins, white craft glue or decoupage medium, scissors, measuring tape, iron and ironing board

HERE'S HOW:

1. Measure the height on the tallest side and perimeter of the box. Add 4" to the height measurement and 2" to the perimeter.
2. Cut the fabric and press to smooth. Position the fabric with one edge flush with the tall end of the box and the "seam" where the two ends will overlap at one corner. Trim the piece to approximately fit the box, leaving enough to fold over and cover the bottom.

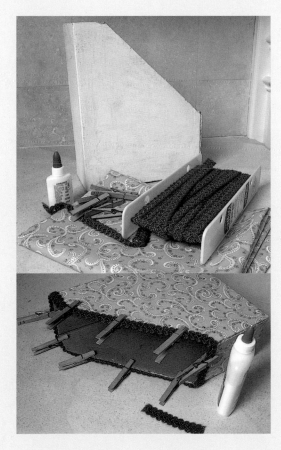

3. Coat one side of the box with glue or decoupage medium and position the fabric with the overlap at the corner. Smooth the fabric in place with fingertips. Follow the same procedure to cover the remaining sides of the box. When you get to the last side, turn under the end so it lines up with the corner.
4. Lay the box on its side. Fold the fabric over the bottom, envelope-style. Trim away excess. Glue the fabric to the bottom of the box. Let dry.
5. Trim the fabric at the top edge flush with the box.
6. Glue braid along the top of the box. Use clothespins to hold the trim in place until the glue is dry. ❏

PLASTIC CONTAINERS

It's hard to beat plastic containers for practicality. They come in all shapes and sizes. You can find large ones that slip under your bed for extra storage, containers for storing food and paper goods, bins for storing toys, and specialized containers for storing CDs, makeup – just about anything!

I like clear plastic containers better than opaque ones unless the containers are going to be stored outside of a closet, drawer, or cabinet. If that's the case, I try to coordinate the color of the boxes or lids with that room's decor. It keeps the space looking more organized and less cluttered. This rule of thumb works well in kid's rooms, playrooms, and even the garage.

I've also started using colored plastic containers for seasonal decorations instead of cardboard boxes. I've noticed over the past few years that stores stock black and orange containers in the fall for Halloween decorations, red and green at Christmas time, and pastels for spring and Easter items. Using seasonal colors means that when I take a trip to the attic or storage space, I can quickly identify the box I want.

Clear plastic shoe boxes can do more than keep your closets neat and tidy; they also make playroom cleanup fast and easy. Give your children several of these shoeboxes and let them help you sort small toys, games, and art supplies into separate boxes. If they're old enough, let them use colored paint pens to label each box. If they are too small to read and write, help them draw simple pictures that denote each box's contents.

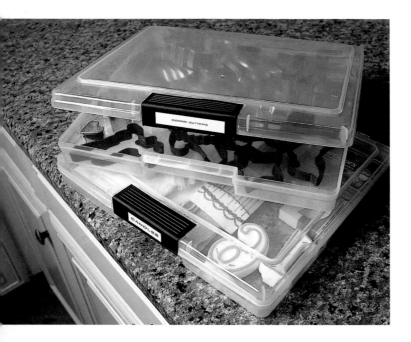

Pictured above: These clear plastic files boxes are the kind sold in scrapbooking departments. They have convenient hinged lids and store flat. I found them great for storing some baking supplies in my pantry. If you only use your cookie cutters, cake decorating supplies, and muffin tins during the holidays, put them in a container and get them down when it's time to make Christmas cookies with the kids. This way, they are out of your way the rest of the year (not taking up drawer space in the kitchen better devoted to items you use every day) but easy to access any time you decide to make cookies. Another container holds birthday candles and items to decorate a cake. The containers can be stacked and stored on the top shelf in the pantry, in an upper cabinet or the bottom of a deep drawer, or on a shelf in the basement or the garage.

Benefits & Considerations

Round Tubs
Benefits:
- Open containers help organize toys, sporting equipment, gardening supplies, laundry, and large projects.
- Sturdy handles let you transport even heavy loads with ease.

Considerations:
- Since they don't have lids, it's hard to stack them or keep out dirt and dampness.
- Not very stylish.

Small Containers
Benefits:
- Ones with lids that seal are great for storing food and items that needs to be kept dry.
- Come in a wide variety of colors and well as clear so you can select the right one for the job.

- Available in round and square shapes for easy stacking to maximize storage space.

Consideration:

- Can break and split if dropped.

Storage Bins

Benefits:

- You can store lots of any type of item in them.
- Wide variety of sizes and shapes.

- Come in clear as well as solid colors for seasonal coordination.
- Most have snap-on lids and handles for easy carrying.
- Keep contents dry and dust free.

Consideration:

- Utilitarian appearance – best kept inside closets or in the attic, basement, or garage.

NEW USES FOR A TREASURED COLLECTION

Rather than storing things away, another option is to keep your eyes open to unconventional ways to use and display your keepsakes and collections. Here, glass and metal frogs – the glass and metal devices placed in vases to hold individual flower stalks in floral arrangements – are displayed on a table to artfully contain arrangements of paint and stencil brushes, markers, and colored pencils.

LABELING

Labeling is essential for file folders and food storage containers, and having labels on opaque containers like boxes and bins makes it easier to locate and retrieve what you're looking for without opening the containers. Labels can be simple or elaborate, utilitarian or decorative.

A label maker like this one pictured below is a specialized machine that allows you to create customized self-adhesive labels on special paper that is resistant to water, spills, heat, cold, and harsh environments. You can also use label making software and print custom labels on your computer printer.

Labels can be simple or elaborate,

utilitarian or decorative.

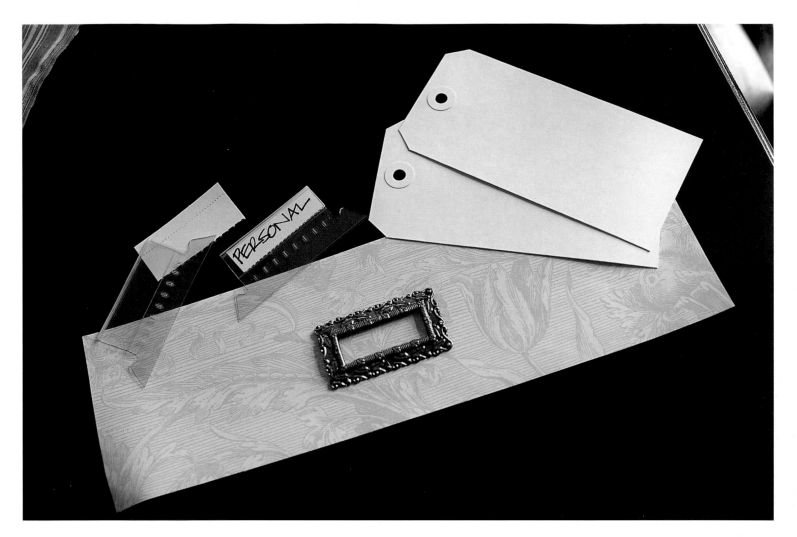

Pictured above: For some applications, the obvious works best, like the plastic holders for the paper tabs that label hanging file folders. For items stored on hangers, take a cue from retail stores and use a hanging tag. Decorative label holder frames can be glued to a variety of surfaces to hold paper labels. You can also find screw-on label holders for wooden surfaces. Card-weight paper can be cut to size to fit label holders. Use a permanent marker to write on labels, print them on a label maker or on a computer, or use rubber stamps.

Pictured left: Handwritten tags label tablecloths by color and size. Simply attach the tag with a safety pin to a corner or edge of the tablecloth for easy identification. Place the cloths in the drawer with the labels on one edge for easy selection.

CHAPTER 2

Organizing
YOUR
Entryway

Where better to start than the front door! It's the first part of the house you see on your way in and the last place you pass through on your way out – for your family and guests as well. If you, like most of us, have two entrances, a front door and a back door, your organization will be based on how you use them. In some homes, for example, the family mainly uses the back door and the front door is reserved for guests and deliveries. In other homes, all the people come and go from the front door and the back door is mainly used by dogs and cats. Take a few minutes to consider the place(s) where your family members exit on their mad dash to life's challenges every day and enter when the day is done.

If your whole house is a complete mess but your front hall or entry is stylish, clean, and well-maintained, you can open the door with confidence, no matter who's arriving. Take the time to tackle this area first.

Pictured opposite page: If you have room, furniture can help establish a warm and inviting entry and provide necessary organization. A small table can be a point of organization in an entry hall. The lamp gives off a warm, inviting glow. A tray on the table holds sunglasses and mail. A wall-hung mirror provides one last look as you dash out the door.

STRATEGY

- Store only the things you need as you come and go from your home.

- Use furniture for storage if you have room. A chest or desk with drawers can be used to stash the daily mail, the dog's leash, your gloves, and your car keys. A coat tree can hold coats, umbrellas, and hats.

- If you don't have a separate entry hall, use the wall space around the door for storage. Look for boxes, shelves, baskets or pockets that can be hung on the wall. Hooks can be the solution for anyone's entryway, formal or casual.

- If you have an entry closet, consider adding hooks on the inside of the door so you can hang items quickly without looking for a hanger.

- You want this area as clutter-free as possible. Don't use the entryway or furniture you've placed there to store objects like clothes or games or cameras. (We'll find places for them in other parts of the house.)

- Designate a place to hold incoming and outgoing mail.

A PLACE FOR MAIL

We get mail almost every day – the good, the bad, and the junk. Use your entry hall – the place where the mail enters the house – to separate the junk from the mail you want to read. Keep a paper recycling container by the door; as you sort through the daily mail you can pitch the junk before it gets farther than the front door. Don't let the entryway be the final destination for the daily mail.

In this chapter you'll find strategies for dealing with mail you want and need to keep in the section on "Organizing Your Home Office," but for now let's focus on jettisoning the junk.

Americans receive over 4,000,000 tons of junk mail each year, and much of it ends up in landfills. You can help reduce

Don't let the entryway

the amount of junk mail you have to sort through everyday by taking a few minutes to get your name removed from the junk mail circuit. Numerous companies keep records on you, and companies buy and sell personal information about you for marketing and other purposes. Anytime you send in a

Pictured left: An attractive wall organizer can hold incoming and outgoing mail.

warranty card, sign up for a mailing list, or enter a contest, your name gets put in a computer somewhere and will eventually end up in the hands of someone that wants to sell you something.

The Direct Marketing Association's (DMA) Mail Preference Service lets you opt out of receiving direct mail marketing from many national companies for five years. When registered with this service, your name will be put on

toll-free number that enables you to "opt out" of having pre-approved credit offers sent to you for two years. Call 1-888-5-OPTOUT (1-888-567-8688) for more information. In addition, you can notify the three major credit bureaus (Equifax, Experian, and TransUnion) that you do not want personal information about you shared for promotional purposes. This action can help eliminate unsolicited mail.

be the final destination for the daily mail.

a "delete" list and made available to direct-mail marketers. To register, send a letter to the Direct Marketing Association, Mail Preference Service, P.O. Box 643, Carmel, NY 10512.

Some junk mail can be dangerous if you don't properly dispose of it. All those pre-approved credit card offers you receive should be shredded or cut up before you toss them to prevent identity theft. To stop unsolicited credit card offers, there is an easy, free solution. The credit bureaus offer a

Pictured above: A bench in an entry hall provides a place to put items while you take off your coat and a place to sit while you change your shoes or sort the mail. It's also a great place to pile guests' coats if you don't have a coat closet (or if your coat closet is full). Use the space under the bench for an attractive basket. Use the basket to hold hats or scarves, clothes headed for the dry cleaner, canvas totes for shopping – any items in transition.

CONTAINERS TO ORGANIZE YOUR COMINGS & GOINGS

Having a particular location to place the items you need to pick up as you're on your way out or put down on your way in will make coming and going from your home easier and less stressful. To keep things organized, choose an attractive container that can hold your loose change, a checkbook and pen, a shopping list, notes or reminders, your keys, the mail, or sunglasses, or gloves – whatever suits your purposes.

Four options for tabletops:

A ceramic bowl is paired with a ceramic pitcher. Attractive in its own right, the pitcher can also be used to hold flowers.

An oval clear glass tray has clean contemporary lines and affords a view of the table covering beneath it.

A woven straw tray is a natural, casual, inexpensive alternative.

Pictured opposite: A silver tray, liberated from storage to gleam in the lamplight, is a more formal option.

HOOKS

Hooks give you a place to hang coats, purses, and umbrellas quickly before they hit the floor and become uncontrolled clutter. And hooks are a great way to get the less organized members of the family to at least make the effort to pick up after themselves, but to train them to be tidy, you have to provide the hook. You could also install hooks on the inside of the coat closet door or inside the closet for hanging guests' coats.

This comfortable spot, *pictured at right,* makes great use of the end of a hallway and showcases a treasure trove of storage solutions. The backdrop of dark-stained wood paneling provides textural interest and defines the space. Metal hooks hold totes and jackets; some are purposefully left empty for guests' belongings. Color-coordinated pillows in sturdy fabrics and an upholstered cushion for sitting can be changed with the seasons. Three low drawers stow kids' gear out of sight but close at hand. A shelf supported by brackets holds baskets for easy access by taller family members. A clock on the wall keeps everyone on schedule.

To train them to be tidy, you have to provide the hook.

CLOSETS

Your entry closet may have been designed just for guests' jackets – don't we all wish we had that much extra space? Truth is, we need that entry closet for our own grab-it-on-the-way-out-the-door jackets and gear.

If you have a shelf or shelves, use baskets to store groups of items. Give each family member a basket or separate items in baskets by category (hats, scarves, gloves). Or use shelf dividers – they are a great way to keep stacks of caps, gloves, and scarves from falling over and getting jumbled together.

You can also use a divided laundry hamper for entry closet storage in the space below hanging jackets. Assign the sections to categories (sports equipment, yoga gear, pet supplies, rain gear) and label them. Or put a shoe rack in the bottom of the closet to store boots or outdoor shoes.

Remember to keep a section with some hangers available for guests!

Closets, continued

The Entry Closet

For optimal functionality, keep your entry closet current with the season. To that end, make a practice of periodically removing all the jackets, hats, gloves, shoes, and coats you're not using in the current season and store them elsewhere. Do the same with gear like tennis racquets, unless you play indoors year-round. (The principle at work here is to keep only currently used items in this closet.)

As you sort through the out-of-season items, be ruthless! Get rid of any item that you did not use during the past season – there's no use in storing something you're not using. Unused items take up much needed space and make you feel guilty that you bought them in the first place. Who needs that? The good feeling you'll have should be sufficient motivation to take 15 minutes and organize that closet.

Pictured opposite page: If your entry closet has to do double or triple duty, like storing the vacuum or a broom in addition to coats and sports gear, install a wall hanger that will give this item its own storage spot. Once it has been used it can easily be returned to its special place. This entry closet is adjacent to the dining room, so it is used to store tablecloths. Each tablecloth is tagged with size and hung on a wooden hanger.

15 minutes in the coat closet:

A SEASONAL MAKEOVER

GATHER:

3 large plastic storage containers or tubs

Sturdy wooden hangers and/or sturdy plastic hangers, 1 color for each family member

GO:

1. Use the three plastic storage tubs to hold things you're not currently using as you remove them from the coat closet – one tub for donations, another for out-of-season items, and a third for any items that need to be moved elsewhere in the house or to the attic or garage.

2. Place the remaining items on matching, sturdy hangers.

   • Use wooden hangers if you prefer them.

   • If multiple family members use this space, select plastic hangers in different colors. Let each child choose a favorite color for his or her coats. Give each child a basket in the same color as the hangers to help keep that child's items together.

   • Don't add additional hangers (unless, of course, you need them for guests' coats). They only encourage you to store additional stuff.

3. Put the donations tub in your car to drop off at a charity or resale shop. Store out-of-season and other items. ❑

CHAPTER 3

Organizing
YOUR
Dining Room

Dining rooms generally aren't just for dining. Is your dining room used for everyday meals or reserved for special dinners? Is this a room where you entertain? Do the kids do their homework at the dining room table or is it the place where you do arts and crafts projects? This chapter addresses storing items traditionally used in dining rooms – dishes, glassware, flatware, and table linens.

STRATEGY

- First ask yourself "What does my family do in this room?" Once you identify how the space is used, you can start organizing it.

- If your dining room is a multi-purpose space, consider using some of the great new storage systems designed specifically for crafts supplies — there are systems for scrapbooking, sewing, and painting, for example. Many of these storage systems are made of canvas, will hold a ton of supplies, and come with rollers that will let you transport them to a nearby closet or to another out-of-the-way storage area. See the section on "Organizing Your Crafts Room" for more about them.

- Storing extraneous items elsewhere frees up your dining room for dining and frees up the storage space in the room for dishes, glassware, serving pieces, and linens. Organizing these items will make them easier to find so you can use them and enjoy them more often.

- Storage goals include protecting fragile items from breakage and storing table linens so wrinkles are kept to a minimum.

CHINA CABINET

A china cabinet is designed to organize, display, and protect your china, stemware, and serving pieces. China cabinets take many guises. A cabinet with glass doors keeps pieces in view but protected from dust; one with solid doors can be arranged without regard to appearances. Some have drawers that can hold flatware or linens. A cabinet with doors and drawers and an open shelf or shelves for display is called a hutch.

An **armoire** can pose as a china cabinet. This type of furniture piece is great if you need maximum storage space. Antique or new, it can provide lots of possibilities for storage and add charm to any dining room. You can dress up a plain armoire by placing full length mirrors on the front doors to reflect the dining experience and add light and an illusion of space. Decorative wood molding can frame out the mirror panels.

continued on page 36

15-minute
CHINA CABINET ORGANIZATION

GATHER:
A quilt or blanket
Furniture polish
Glass cleaner
Soft rags and paper towels

GO:
1. Cover your dining table with a quilt or blanket to protect the surface while you organize.
2. Move everything from the china cabinet to your table, grouping items by color and function.
3. Clean your cabinet well.
4. Return the items to your cabinet, dusting or cleaning items as necessary. *If your cabinet has glass doors,* create an interesting presentation by arranging pieces that are the same color together and using easels to display large platters and bowls. *If your cabinet has solid doors,* stack the items according to use. Put all pieces of each set of dishes together. Store glasses stem end up to keep out dust. Group larger serving pieces together on one shelf. ❑

China Cabinets, continued

Inside the armoire, drawers and shelves inside allow lots of room for customization. You can store dishes in stacks to maximize your space. Do not stack dishes more than 6" high. Too tall a stack will put excess weight on the bottom dishes and can cause breakage. Store silverware in tarnish resistant storage boxes or cases. Table linens can be laid flat and in stacks on shelves to eliminate wrinkles.

CHESTS OF DRAWERS

If you only have room for one additional piece of furniture in your dining room, make it a chest of drawers. I love using one in addition to (or even instead of) the more traditional china cabinet. Chests of drawers are versatile storage pieces that keep your items safe, clean, and ready to use. In addition, it can be used as a buffet or extra surface to hold a wine bottle, dessert, etc.

Whether this chest of drawers is a bedroom dresser, a highboy, a sideboard, a hunt table, or a buffet, make sure the piece you select isn't too tall – you want to be able to use the top for serving and display. Check the drawers. Do they pull out easily? Are they sturdy? You need drawers that can carry heavy loads of dishes and silverware and still open and close with ease after years of use.

- Use the upper drawers for easy access to napkins, napkin rings, and flatware.
- Use lower drawers for tablecloths and placemats, organized by color.
- To distribute the weight, store a few dishes and a few linens in each drawer.
- Place a lamp on your chest of drawers to provide indirect illumination in the dining room.

ORGANIZING DISHES

I love dishes, and I can't help but be captivated by their charm, but storing them takes up a lot of space. As with any hobby or passion, organization aids enjoyment. Organization begins with weeding out what you don't need or want, and your dish collection is no exception. Here are some questions to ask yourself as you sort out your dish collection.

Do I Love It?

Every dish and glass you keep should be one you really like – one that makes you smile when you see it on your table.

How Many Do I Need?

Inventory the number of place settings you have in each set. How many you need depends on the size of your family, how many people can comfortably be seated at your table, and how sentimental you are about the dishes in question. For me, eight is a good minimum number of place settings to

Organization aids enjoyment

15-minute
ORGANIZING TIPS

Tip #1 – Make an Inventory

Get a notebook and make a written inventory of your dishes. As you organize and put away your dishes, note on your inventory sheet where you store each set of dishes and serving pieces. (If you can't find them, you can't use them.) Keep your notebook in the pantry and/or stash it on the shelf next to your favorite cookbook.

Tip #2 – Use Storage Containers

Purchase storage cases for each dish collection. Buying cases for everything in the same color may look very stylish, but coordinating the color of the case with the pattern or color of the dishes can help you find what you're looking for much quicker. (It only takes an extra five to ten minutes to get out the "good china" if you know where it is.)

Label storage containers with the name of the pattern, the type of dish, and the number of pieces contained inside. This way, if you are having a dinner for eight people you won't waste time getting out a set with only six place settings.

Tip #3 – Change with the Seasons

Rotate dishes based on seasons. Use light and pastel colors in spring and summer, darker earth tones in fall and winter and red and gold for holidays and special occasions. Store out-of-season colors in upper cabinets or on the top shelves of your pantry or guest room closet.

Tip #4 – Use One Color of Dishes

Collect only one color of dishes and serving pieces, then sort by shape and use. (That color doesn't have to be white.)

Tip #5 – Organize by Use

Put the items you use the most in the most accessible space. (If you eat cereal every day, put the cereal bowls where you can reach them easily. If you make a salad every day for dinner, keep the salad bowl in a convenient spot.)

have in any dish set. I give away sets of dishes with fewer than four place settings, but that's a personal choice. If you really love their color or shape and you really need a dish just that size, keep one or two serving pieces or keep a special plate to use when you eat lunch alone. Donate the rest. (That's one reason I love dishes – they get passed from one family to another, perhaps eventually arriving at my house.)

Is It in Good Condition?

Any dish or glass that is chipped, bent, missing something (like a lid), or is stained is a candidate for tossing.

Can I Get It Fixed or Get More?

If you are missing a cup or two, or if one or more plates are chipped, decide if this dish set is worth keeping. If it is, have the chipped pieces repaired or buy replacements. You can find companies that specialize in restoration and replacements on the Internet.

Storing China If You Don't Have a China Cabinet

If you have a large china cabinet or storage closet where you can store all your dishes on shelves, lucky you! But most of us don't have that much space and must depend on remote storage (a location away from the dining room or kitchen).

Pack and label dishes you don't use every day in storage containers (see Organizing Tip #2) and place the containers inside a sturdy clear plastic tub. Label the tub with a number, and note that number in your inventory notebook (see Organizing Tip #1). Store the tub(s) in the garage, pantry, and/or guest room closet. When it's time for a party (or you're ready for a change), check your inventory list and retrieve those dishes – they'll be clean and ready to use; you'll just have to set the table.

Wash them after the party, and when they are thoroughly dry, pack them away in their containers. Put the containers in the tub(s) and store until the next occasion.

ORGANIZING FLATWARE

You need two main sets of flatware, one for everyday use and another for special occasions. Sort accordingly.

Store special silverware in tarnish-proof cabinets, drawers, chests, or roll-up cases. Roll-up cases minimize the space required for storage. Stack them in a basket for easy transport to the dining table.

Everyday flatware should be kept in a drawer near the dishwasher or the table or snack bar – wherever your family eats most meals. To maximize storage space, determine the number of space divisions you need. Measure your drawer, then buy dividers to fit inside the drawer or buy a kit and build your own dividers. (The kit is a great option if you have odd-sized drawers or want to put dividers in the drawer of a piece of antique furniture.)

ORGANIZING TABLE LINENS

I love the feel of beautiful, smooth table linens. Proper storage is the key to always having a fresh, wrinkle-free, tablecloth and napkins ready for use. Linens store best if they aren't put in deep stacks – piling them up encourages crease marks. They also need circulating air to keep them fresh, so be sure to give them room to breathe. Write the dimensions of table-cloths on easily visible tags and pin them on the edge. You'll be able to choose the right size cloth without unfolding.

Pictured below: Storing a tablecloth on a hanger.

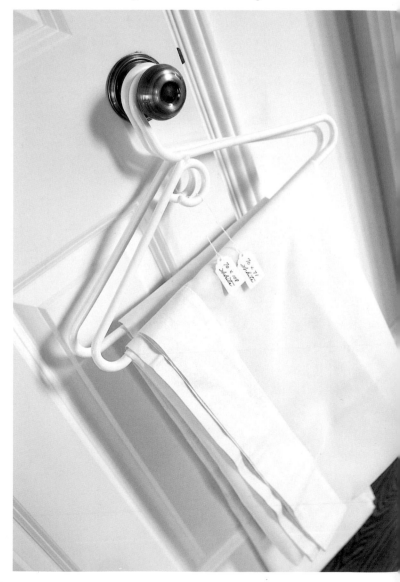

Storage Options for Tablecloths & Placemats

- **A dresser.** I replaced my traditional china cabinet with a large bedroom dresser. The drawers are wide and deep, allowing me to store linens flat and with as few folds as possible. If you don't have the space in the dining room or can't part with Aunt Sally's antique Duncan Phyfe hutch, put this dresser in the guest room, hallway, or basement.

- **An armoire.** An armoire can be used for table linens if you add additional shelving. (See how to do this in the section "Organizing Bedrooms & Personal Spaces.")

- **On rolls or bolts.** You can store tablecloths by rolling them around round fabric rolls or folding them around the cardboard rectangles that bolts of fabric come on. (Ask your local fabric shop if they will give or sell you these items.) Rolls and bolts can be stored upright in the corner of a closet or stacked side by side on a closet shelf.

- **On hangers.** I have my best tablecloths dry cleaned the morning after the party. It is more affordable than you think, and I'm amazed by the cleaners' incredible ability to remove red wine, grease, and lipstick stains from white linen. My cleaner returns them on a wide hanger with a cardboard roll. I keep those hangers and use them for storing my washable everyday table linens.

Storing Napkins

Keep sets of napkins together and store them flat or folded once in a drawer. That way, you can fold them for the table without ironing. Roll everyday napkins if space is limited.

Pictured above right: Tablecloth labels make it easy to find the size you need.

Pictured right: Napkin storage.

CHAPTER 4

Organizing
YOUR
Kitchen

"Order and cleanliness must reign in the kitchen; everything must be in its place, well polished, well cleaned," declared *La Parfaite Cuisiniere bourgeoisie et economique* in 1853. We're still trying to live up to that standard.

Most of us blame our organizational failures on the size of our kitchens. ("My kitchen is too small." "I don't have a pantry." "There's not adequate storage space.") But most of us do have plenty of storage space if we get rid of unused items, get organized, and make efficient use of our space. Sounds simple, doesn't it?

STRATEGY

- Working one cabinet or drawer at a time, examine what you're storing in your kitchen. Do you use it? Do you need it? Do you want it? If the answer is no, eliminate it! Pass it along, give it away, or have a yard sale.

- Make a place for everything you need to store. Explore customized options and different types of containers.

- Store items you use the most often on the easiest-to-reach shelves.

- Place items you use less often on higher shelves. Group similar types of items in see-through plastic bins that you can label and access easily.

- Keep heavy things on lower shelves.

- Use the top of the refrigerator. Put a large wicker basket on top and fill it with extra dishtowels, large serving bowls, or other items that you don't use every day.

LINEN STORAGE

Store linens you use at the kitchen table or breakfast bar in a kitchen cabinet rather than a drawer. Cabinets are typically larger than drawers, so you'll have less folding and wrinkling to deal with, and everything's visible at a glance – there's no rooting around for what you want. Having pullout, tray-type shelves for larger items like tablecloths and placemats makes them easier to access.

Pictured opposite page: An otherwise unused space beside the backdoor benefits from this narrow shelving unit. A basket holds tea towels so they are always at the ready. Glass containers hold citrus fruit.

LARGE PLATTER & TRAY STORAGE

Trays and platters are easier to access if they are stored standing on one edge instead of stacked. This cabinet with dividers makes full use of the space above a refrigerator.

HERBS, SPICES & CONDIMENTS

They come in small bottles, jars, and cans in a variety of shapes colors, and sizes. Some containers are attractive, some are simply utilitarian, and some should just be kept out of sight. Organizationally, herbs, spices, and condiments present challenges. Their small size means they can easily get lost in cabinets and on deep shelves. Often, we end up keeping lots of them close at hand in plain sight, like on a counter or near the stove – even items we don't use all that often, such as a bottle of vanilla (only for baking) or a tin of crab boil (only for seasoning fish). Here are some ideas for organizing them:

- **Choose a good spot.** Since spices and herbs lose their flavors when exposed to moisture, light, and heat, keep them in tightly closed containers away from windows and hot spaces (e.g., don't store them above the stove).

- **Go shopping.** Lots of great spice racks – some meant to be used inside cabinets or drawers, others that can sit on counters or be hung on the wall – are available at kitchen shops and from catalogs.

- **Use a drawer.** Try using a shallow drawer instead of a shelf. Lay the containers side-by-side in the drawer. You can quickly access your spices without taking up valuable shelf space better used for dishes and glassware. And storing them in closed jars in a drawer, away from light, makes them last longer.

- **Foster uniformity.** Consider purchasing containers that are all the same style or size and use a professional label machine to make attractive, easy-to-read labels.

- **Buy big, store small.** I buy the spices I use most often in bulk at warehouse stores. I pour a small amount in the kitchen storage container and store the large jar in the pantry. But don't buy spices in bulk unless you can use up your supply in less than six months. After that, most spices lose their spunk!

- **Group messy stuff.** Sticky and messy cooking ingredients like mustard, syrup, liquid flavorings are best stored on trays, in a shallow plastic bin, or on a lazy Susan in a cabinet, pantry, or refrigerator. When the bottom of the bin or tray gets messy (and it will), it's much easier to take it to the sink and wash it (or run it through the dishwasher, even) than to clean the shelf it sits on. Your surfaces will be free of pepper sprinkles and sticky honey drips.

- **Line them up.** Store foodstuffs that come in small containers one deep on wall-hung narrow shelves or racks in the pantry. (More on pantries follows.)

Pictured above: A pretty two-tiered pedestal holds a jumble of small containers. Even though the containers are utilitarian and of varied sizes, they look acceptable when grouped. The charm of the pedestal helps – and it is placed near the stove for easy access.

15-minute
ORGANIZED JUNK DRAWER

Every family has a junk drawer – it's the place where all the things that don't have a home end up. To function optimally as a temporary storage spot, the junk drawer needs to be cleaned out every so often. If you do this faithfully, your junk drawer will only have good, useful everyday junk. What a great improvement!

1. Remove everything from the drawer that already has a home. Miscellaneous papers, receipts, unlabeled keys, hair accessories, and sunglasses don't belong in the junk drawer. Remove them! Put them where they belong.
2. Take a cardboard box large enough to allow sorting. Dump the contents of the drawer in the box and sort through it.

Before you put anything back in the drawer, ask yourself, "Is there a better place for this item?" Chances are carry-out menus from your favorite restaurants would be more accessible if you kept them in a folder with pockets inside the cabinet near the phone or in the home office. Items like batteries or light bulbs can (and should) be stored all together in one box.

3. Keep what's left in the box, put the box in a central location, and announce to your family, "Take what you want before midnight tomorrow. All that remains will be thrown out." You'll be amazed how quickly the junk will disappear! (If it doesn't, be strong and pitch it yourself.) ❏

PANTRY

The pantry can become the most disorganized space in the house very quickly. Remember when you played store with that plastic food you got with your first toy kitchen – you had one egg, one slice of bread, and one carton of milk. It's not that simple anymore. We over-buy. We forget. Sometimes food doesn't get eaten because we can't find it – when we discover it, it's often past its prime.

To keep a pantry organized it is necessary for you to take the time to measure everything you want to store, install the correct shelves, racks, and holders, and invest in see-through containers in various sizes that work for what you want to store.

Pictured right: Clear, airtight storage jars keep foods fresher, and they are easier to organize than an array of open packages. Besides, open packages appeal to insects – enough said.

Pantry, continued

Store foods in your pantry by categories, just like the grocery store does. Put your "big sellers" (the things you use most often) on the middle shelves, the heavy items on the bottom, and the tall, light items (unopened boxes of cereal, snacks in bags) and things you use less often on the top shelves. This makes it really easy to see what you have to cook with and what you are missing. Leave space for the items that you will be restocking if you are out of them.

Place smaller items in baskets or bins so you can access them easily and they won't get lost on the shelf or tucked to the back of deep shelves. Use floral buckets or baskets to store potatoes, onions, apples, and other produce that doesn't require refrigeration.

Use the same guidelines for storing non-food items like picnic items, paper plates, foil pans, and baking supplies. Group like items in see-through plastic bins or zipper-top plastic bags so you can locate them easily and they'll stay clean and ready for use. Label everything.

Recycle extra paper sacks and plastic bags. These items have a way of accumulating much faster than we can use them. If you do have lots of uses for those plastic grocery bags, consider installing an attractive dispenser/storage container on the wall.

Continued on page 52

Pictured above: Grouping items you don't use every day in plastic bins and labeling them makes them easier to locate when you want them.

Pictured left: Store infrequently used items in baskets or bins on upper shelves.

Pictured opposite page: When you store food items in attractive plastic or glass containers rather than their original packaging, it is quick and easy to assemble a beautiful self-serve breakfast bar for overnight guests. (Foods stay fresh longer, too.)

Pantry, continued

Once you have your pantry properly outfitted and the containers are ready and handy, you can keep your pantry organized and functional by spending 15 minutes whenever disorganization starts showing up.

How to Re-Organize Food in a Pantry

1. **Survey.** Take a minute to see what is out of place. Is there a pattern here? Maybe you need to change the layout of your pantry. If every time you re-organize the same items are in the wrong place, maybe they are trying to tell you something. You may need to adjust your layout to better meet your family's needs.

2. **Check the packages.** Look at the packaged food in your pantry. Get a trash can and a paper sack, and take everything out. Keep only food in good condition (check expiration dates on cans and packages) that you know you or someone in your family will actually want to eat. Make each item pass this test. What is more important – having the space the item takes up or the item itself? Toss food that's past its prime in the trash can. Put food you will never use before its expiration date in the paper sack. Place it in your car, and plan to drop it off at your local food bank.

3. **Sort through the produce.** Empty out the vegetable bins, tossing spoiled produce, and brush out any debris.

4. **Fill containers.** Pour the contents of any opened boxes or bags of snacks or chips into re-sealable see-through containers. Arrange them on the shelves. Dispose of food if it's stale or if there's not enough for one serving.

5. **Arrange.** Group food types together with the labels facing forward so you can see what you have. (Out of sight IS out of mind.)

6. Make a list of out-of-stock items so you can take it with you to the store next time you shop. That way, you'll buy what you need, eliminate duplication, and not have too many items to store. ❏

BEVERAGES

It's easy and pleasant to serve hot beverages to family or guests or to treat yourself to a relaxing cup of tea when everything you need is organized and accessible. Store items together in a cabinet or drawer or on a shelf so you can easily assemble a tray that you can carry to the living room, dining room, or porch.

Pictured left: The cabinet above the coffee maker is the ideal place to store canisters of coffee and sugar, jars of powdered creamer, and tins of powdered hot chocolate. Individually wrapped teabags are gathered in a glass container. When guests are about, simply leave the cabinet door open to invite self-serving.

Pictured opposite page: Use a wooden tray to assemble the makings for morning beverages. It's easier for family and friends to prepare their own beverages when everything is in one place. The tray can be left on the kitchen counter and re-supplied and tidied up when needed. Since everything is organized on this portable tray, it is easy to transport to breakfast table, patio, or wherever breakfast is being served.

To assemble the tray, line it with a pretty placemat to catch drips or spills as well as look attractive. Add teabags in boxes and packets, individual envelopes of cocoa mix, a sugar bowl and creamer, a porcelain dish of sweetener packets, individual holders for teabags after use (necessary if you're using cups without saucers). Pour hot water from a ceramic carafe. Have a cloth towel nearby in case it's needed for wiping up.

53

ORGANIZING CABINETS

Storing Dishes & Glassware

If it seems like there's just not enough room in your cabinets for your everyday dishes and glassware, don't despair. A little time spent organizing your cabinet space can yield amazing results. You'll be delighted to rediscover your favorite pieces – it's like getting a whole new kitchen! You

Continued on page 56

Pictured top right: Adding a wire shelf allows additional storage in space between fixed shelves and eliminates precarious stacking.

Pictured bottom right: White plates of various sizes and shapes are stored together in one cabinet. The ones used more often are stored on lower shelves.

Pictured bottom left: Dishes and glassware stored in base cabinets on pullout shelves.

Pictured opposite page: If you have glass-front cabinets, store serving pieces like pitchers, platters, and soup tureens in them so you can enjoy the shapes every day. Grouping items by color makes the cabinets look less cluttered.

Storing Dishes & Glassware, continued

will also be able to assess what pieces you actually need and which ones you need to give away or put away. Begin by eliminating items you're not using (you can store them in bins or boxes elsewhere if you want to keep them, not toss them). Then organize. Here are some ideas:

- **Install a stemware rack.** Use the space under wall cabinets to hang wine glasses, stemmed goblets, and champagne flutes upside-down on a stemware rack attached to the bottom of a cupboard.

- **Group by color.** Regardless of the shape or pattern, divide dishes into color groups rather than by sets. If you display and store all your white dishes together, for example, you will be able to set a complete table from just one cupboard instead of looking throughout the kitchen for bowls, plates, and serving pieces. Because the dishes are all one color, your cupboards will appear more spacious and organized.

- **Install pullout tray-type shelves in base cabinets.** Pullout shelves greatly expand the usability of your base cabinets. You can use them to store any kind of dish or glassware. It's easy to see and retrieve what you want.

- **Add drawers.** If you are remodeling or adding cabinets, consider base cabinets with drawers instead of doors. A drawer puts the contents of the whole cabinet within easy reach.

- **Add some wire shelves.** Take advantage of the entire height of your cabinets. Vinyl-covered wire shelving units, available at home improvement centers and container and hardware stores, are an easy, fast, inexpensive way to provide extra shelf space in cupboards.

- **Don't make stacks too high.** Remember not to stack dishes more than 6" high. Too tall a stack will put excess weight on the dishes on the bottom and cause them to break. Besides, dishes are easier to move around if the stacks aren't too tall.

Pots & Pans & Lids

Pots and pans and all those lids can take up lots (and lots!) of cabinet space. Here are some space-saving ideas:

- **Hang on a rack.** Take a cue from professional kitchens and suspend a sturdy rack from the ceiling to hang pots and pans.

- **Hang on the wall.** A metal wall rack can keep pots and pans within easy reach and clear out overcrowded cabinets.

- **Put pegboard in the pantry.** Install pegboard inside your pantry with hooks to hang and organize your pans. Take a tip from Julia Child's kitchen and trace the outline of each pan on the pegboard – you'll always put it back in its special spot.

Pictured above: Pots and pans stored on sliding shelves in a base cabinet.

Before: A crowded base cabinet. The upper shelf is shallow so some space goes unused. It's hard to reach items in the back of the bottom shelf, and it's hard to see what's back there in the dark.

- **Put lids in a drawer.** Use a drawer to contain lids for saucepans and skillets. To corral lids for plastic storage containers and plastic storage lids for glass baking dishes, place an expandable curtain rod inside a drawer, 2 to 3" from the front edge, and stack the lids on their edges.

- **Use a dish drainer.** Organize pot lids, cookie sheets, and muffin pans in a small dish drainer and place inside a cabinet.

- **Add sliding shelves in base cabinets.** Sliding shelves maximize available space.

After: Pullout shelves bring everything out into the light and within easy reach.

"Order and Cleanliness must reign in the kitchen; everything must be in it's place . . ."

HOW TO INSTALL SLIDING SHELVES

You can buy (online or in stores where kitchen cabinetry is sold) pullout shelves and hardware for installing them to retrofit your existing kitchen cabinets. Disruption is minimal (cabinets stay in place) and much less expensive than installing new cabinets. Sliding shelves are easy to install for the average homeowner and can take as little as five minutes to install. The shelves you buy will come with detailed installation instructions. Following is a brief description of ways to install sliding shelves.

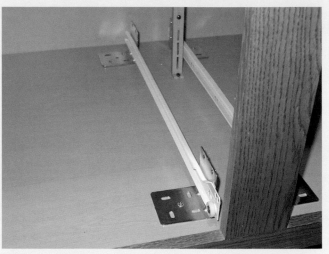

1. Sliding shelves can be mounted in a variety of cabinet styles. They can be mounted to a full base such as the bottom of this cabinet. They can also be mounted to a half shelf as shown in this cabinet. And they can also be installed where there are no shelves at all by using side rear socket mounts or by mounting to the cabinet sides.

2. The easiest installation is when mounting the sliding shelf to the cabinet base or an existing full depth shelf. The slides have L-brackets attached to them. Here the slides for the drawers are in place with the wheels facing forward.

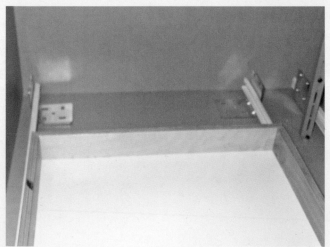

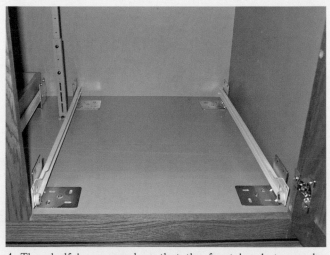

3. The shelf is put in place to make sure the slides are in position. The shelf is pulled out so back brackets are exposed. The back brackets will be screwed in place while shelf is in position.

4. The shelf is removed so that the front brackets can be attached and tightened.

5. Here the bottom shelves are installed and in place.

6. Slides can be mounted on half shelves, but the shelves must be the kind that do not lift – they must be stationery and secure. Here the slides are positioned and leveled.

7. When the slide is level the location of the front hole in the slide is marked. Then the height is measured and a corresponding mark is made on the other side face frame.

8. The slides for both sides are positioned and leveled.

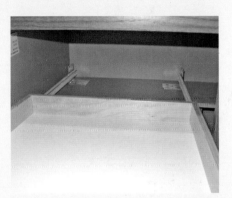

9. The drawer is placed to check the slide positioning before tightening the screws on the L brackets.

10. Here the slides have been mounted and the drawer is in place.

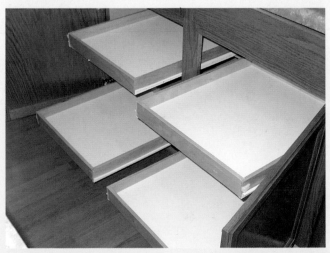

11. Four drawers have been successfully installed in this existing cabinet.

COOKING UTENSILS

Keep and store only those kitchen tools you actually use, and reserve the most accessible storage areas for the items you use most often. Organizing your cooking utensils makes meal preparation so much easier.

- **Store knives on the wall.** Invest in a wall-mounted magnetic strip to store your kitchen knives. It's safer than keeping them loose in a drawer, and they are easy to access while you're cooking. (No more dangerous, frustrating searches for your favorite paring knife. No more nicked and damaged blades.)

- **Use drawer dividers.** Organize and categorize with drawer dividers. Customize drawers with purchased interlocking organizers, or use modular plastic boxes.

- **Use mats.** Cut non-skid rubber mats to size with scissors and place in the bottoms of drawers to keep items from sliding to the back. You can buy matting in rolls at hardware and home improvement centers. Or buy a thin rubber rug pad and cut it up.

Pictured right: Drawer dividers keep utensils in place and accessible.

CLEANING SUPPLIES

Most of us use the space around and under the kitchen sink for storing household cleaning products. Be sure to check containers regularly to make sure they are in good condition. Here are some ideas for keeping your cleaning products organized:

- **Install a sliding basket.** Buy and install a sliding wire basket to hold cleaning products under the sink. You'll be able to see and access products easily, and all those plastic bottles will stand upright so they're less likely to spill or leak.

- **Use a plastic tote.** Organize your cleaning supplies under the sink in a tray-type tote with a handle or a plastic bucket. You can easily remove the tote or bucket and carry it room to room while you clean – you'll have all your supplies organized and with you, saving time and extra trips. The tote also keeps your under-sink cabinet cleaner and protects it from accidental spills and harmful chemicals.

- **Contain plastic bags.** If you store plastic bags for re-use, purchase one of those handy holders or stuff them into an empty facial tissue box for easy access.

- **Install a tilting tray.** To organize sponges, scouring pads, and small brushes, install a hidden, tilting tray in front of your sink to replace the false drawer front. Kits are available at home improvement stores.

- **Be safe!** If you have small children at home, be sure your under-sink cabinet is latched and secure, or store cleaning supplies out of reach in another area.

quick project

CLOTHESPIN MAGNETS

Make your refrigerator your family message center with these colorful magnetic clothespins. (You could also use them to hold recipe cards, schedules, shopping lists, and photos.) Choose a color that coordinates with your kitchen (a single color looks more organized) and label one for each family member.

YOU'LL NEED:

Wooden spring-type clothespins (one for each family member), magnets, white craft glue, acrylic craft paint in the color of your choice, a paintbrush, fine-tip permanent marker.

HERE'S HOW:

1. Dye or paint the wooden clothespins and allow to dry. Dilute paint with water and use a small brush to paint.
2. Write a name on each clothespin with a permanent marker.
3. Glue a magnet to the back of each clothespin. When the glue is dry, they are ready to use. ❏

CHAPTER 5

Storage Solutions
FOR
Entertaining & Decorating
ESSENTIALS

Giving a party, setting a festive table for a dinner party, and serving beverages to friends who drop by are all easier and more pleasant for everyone if what you need is on hand, easy to find, and accessible. Organizing for entertaining means no frantic searching at the last minute for cocktail napkins, a flower vase or candles to create a centerpiece, or dinner music that suits the mood you want to create. And when you want to watch a favorite movie or video with your kids or grandkids, you'll know just where to find them.

VASES

When you need a vase, whether you are decorating for an event or to match a room's decor, it's easy to select just the right size if you organize your vases by color. To get them organized, don't stash your vases all over the house. Collect them from the garage, kitchen, laundry room, and closets. Set them out on a table, group them – all clear ones together, colors separated – and determine the storage space needed for each group.

I use cardboard boxes with dividers (the kind bottles of wine are shipped in) to hold my small vases. I cut down the sides of the boxes to the right height with a utility knife. When I need a vase, I pull out the entire box and find just the one I want without running the risk of their toppling off the shelf and breaking.

Chances are you don't need more than one pair of matching vases, unless you are catering the next family wedding or throwing a graduation party. Clear out the clutter and dispose of duplicate floral containers (like those that come with Internet floral orders). Donate them to churches or community centers so they can be used for weddings, banquets, or other group functions.

Floral Arranging Supplies

Store floral arranging supplies – shears, plant food, frogs, and such – in a rustic container, such as an old wooden fruit crate or tool box or a basket, and keep it in a convenient location. Use berry cartons, glass containers, or recycled tin cans from canned foods to hold wire, floral picks, and other small supplies.

PICNIC ITEMS

quick project

RECYCLED STORAGE TINS

Let your children use acrylic craft paints to decorate clean, empty metal cans and food containers in bright colors. Display them in a basket, tray, or wooden box and let the kids help you sort small supplies and place them in the containers. They'll learn how to organize and you'll contain clutter in minutes while enjoying quality time with your kids.

In the summertime, keep a wooden box or large basket near the porch door filled with things for outdoor meals or an impromptu picnic (colorful napkins, placemats or a tablecloth, salt and pepper shakers, plastic flatware). Making your supplies part of your decor keeps them accessible and makes your home more a reflection of you and your personal style.

CANDLES & CANDLE HOLDERS

Storing all your candles and candle holders in one spot makes it simple to see what candles you have on hand and easy to choose the right holders. Having pullout shelves in a cabinet (like the ones in the photo, below) is ideal. If your cabinet space is more limited, use clear plastic bins with lids for storing supplies and stack them in a closet or in the laundry room. Or place them in deep baskets and put the baskets on top of a bookcase or armoire. Use clear plastic bubble wrap to separate breakable items.

Group taper candles according to color and store each color separately. (If you don't, over time the colors will migrate.) Using wide-mouth jars or glasses holds them upright. I use one jar for all my white and ivory candles and individual jars for holiday reds and oranges.

Don't store candles in hot attics or garages. They will melt.

PARTY SUPPLIES & DECORATIONS

An old cabinet works great for displaying your collection and inspiring your next party. My friend Joyce has organized her paper products in an armoire – just opening the door makes you think about giving a party. Drawers also are great for storing napkins. It's very handy to have a drawer or cabinet near the area where you serve beverages.

An easy way to sort through and organize paper products is by seasons. Put all the colors and themes together, regardless of the item's purpose. If cabinet space is limited, store each group in a see-through plastic bag or container and put it away until its season rolls around. Instead of letting all those bargain napkins and paper plates go unpurchased at the end of the season, develop an organized storage system and stock up when prices are low.

Pictured right: Party Supplies and decorations are arranged on armoire shelves.

Cocktails & Refreshments

It is so much easier to entertain friends who drop in when you have a well-organized wet bar and serving area.

- **Store glasses** in cabinets to keep them clean and dust free.
- **Use a drawer organizer** to separate bar tools, cocktail napkins, and decorative accessories like bottle stoppers.
- **Inventory your drinks** (wines, aperitifs, mixers, liquor). Make a list of what you need to buy next time you shop.
- **Use a tray** to keep items organized and displayed on top of the counter. The tray can also be used for serving.
- **Be safe!** Store alcohol in a locked cabinet if you have underage children living at home or visiting frequently.

Pictured left: A pullout shelf under a bar sink holds bottles upright.

A cabinet serves as a bar area in a family room. A pull-out drawer in the cabinet holds cocktail napkins, bottle openers, coasters, and other tools needed when serving beverages. A wooden tray on top of cabinet holds open wine bottles, glasses, and napkins, ready for serving.

MEDIA STORAGE

Get a basket large enough to contain all the remotes (or purchase one remote that operates multiple units) and a small flashlight. Give it a home – on a shelf, on the coffee table, inside your entertainment center. If you have frequent guests who use your equipment, use color-coordinated stick-on dots to identify a remote and its corresponding machine.

Videotapes, DVDs, CDs, and other media materials can be stored in boxes (wood, cardboard, plastic), bins, baskets, or trays for easy handling and categorizing. When planning your storage solutions, keep these dimensions in mind:

Videotape – 7-1/2" x 4-1/8"

CD/DVD – 5" x 5-5/8"

Audio cassette – 4-1/4" x 2-3/4"

15-minute project

ORGANIZE YOUR VIDEOS

Unlabeled videotapes are accidents waiting to happen – you don't want to accidentally tape over the kids' favorite movie or your wedding video. Take 15 minutes every so often to label all the unmarked videos. (If you have lots of them, it may take several 15-minutes sessions to get them under control, but persevere.)

Use different colors of markers to quickly color code by viewer appeal – red for kid's titles, blue for adults', and green for general family viewing, for example.

GATHER:

Your videos, a sheet of computer labels, 3 colors of markers, storage boxes or baskets

GO:

1. Pop a tape into the VCR long enough to identify it (no more than that – now is not the time to travel down memory lane!). Remove it.
2. *If the video is one you want to keep,* stick on a label and write a title on the label, using the designated marker color. Place it in a storage box or basket. *If you don't want to save what's recorded,* set it aside.
3. Repeat until 15 minutes is up or you've finished all the videos. Put all the videos you've set aside in a box or basket labeled "For re-recording." ❏

Bin-style baskets can hold remote controls and videotapes.

An old wooden paper tray is an attractive storage option for compact discs.

FOR THE FAMILY ROOM

Get everyone in the family involved in an easy pick-up game to help keep your family room or living room organized. When everything has a home and tasks have been assigned, an entire room can be put in order in just minutes a day.

1. **Make a place for everything.** Discuss where everything is going to be stored and make sure there is a place for every item that gets used on a daily or weekly basis. Take suggestions from your family, for example, as to the best place to keep the remotes, the daily newspapers, magazines, throws, toys, and pillows.

2. **Assign everyone a task.** Make the assignment match with who uses those items the most. If it's the newspaper and Dad is the daily reader, make it his job to pick up the paper at the end of the day and place it in the recycling bin. If you're the magazine reader, put them in baskets placed on shelves or under the coffee table. If your kids use the family room as a playroom, here's a way to manage their toys. Purchase a round plastic storage bin in each child's favorite color. Designate a time each day, like after dinner before bedtime, when the kids are responsible for picking up their toys and putting away their bins in a designated location. If space allows, place a decorative screen across one corner of the room and store the toy bins behind the screen.

Ideally, take 15 minutes and do this every day. (It also works when company is coming or you just can't take the clutter any longer.)

Tip: The best way to keep food and dirty dishes from collecting in the family room is to establish a no eating zone. Confine eating to the kitchen, the dining room table, or outside (during the warm weather). Then it will be a special treat on Friday night to enjoy popcorn and a soda while watching a movie with the family.

Pictured left: Labeled clear plastic bins keep videos organized, visible, and dust-free.

CHAPTER 6

Organizing Bedrooms & Personal Spaces

Including sleeping, relaxing, and getting dressed, we spend nearly half our lives in our bedrooms and adjacent personal spaces. The bedroom is where we store our most personal possessions, and it's the place where we can shut out the world by closing the door.

STRATEGY

- **Bed.** Always make your bed. It is the easiest and fastest way to make your bedroom look organized. When the day is over and you're ready for bed, you have the reward of a nice, orderly bed. When at least this part of your disorganized house is orderly, all will seem right with the world.

- **Closets.** Whenever possible, hang everything. But remember the phrase attributed to Joan Crawford, "No more wire hangers!" Replace them with plastic or wooden ones. Install an expansion rod a few inches from the ceiling and use S-hooks to hang handbags and totes to keep them off your shelves or floor. Or hang a pot rack from the ceiling to store purses. Keep only clothes you're actually wearing in your closet. The goal is simple: A great outfit you feel good about wearing.

- **Shelving Units and Dressers.** Clothes can be folded and placed on shelves or in dressers. If there is room in your closet, place an old dresser with drawers against an empty wall or under a tall clothes rod. Use it for underwear, socks, and sweats. Baskets, boxes, and bins can be stored on shelves and used like drawers.

- **Armoires.** An armoire or an entertainment center is the perfect way to organize a disorganized bedroom. If you need maximum storage space, an armoire can be the ticket. Some units designed for the family room work great in a bedroom. Buy as large a piece as space will allow. It can be used as a cabinet for the television as well as provide shelf space for clothing, accessories or linens. Using baskets on the shelves to hold items makes organization easier.

- **Nightstand:** It is essential to have a piece of furniture next to the bed to hold a lamp, reading material, tissues, glasses, and other personal items. Ones with both shelves and at least one drawer are most functional. Nightstands don't always have to be traditional pieces of furniture. A small table such as a metal garden table, a wooden chair with a nice flat seating surface, or even a substantial stack of books with a glass table-top can be used as a nightstand.

Pictured right: Labeled boxes with lids offer a sleek, modern look for storing wearables.

Pictured opposite page: The furniture in this bedroom offers many storage options. The nightstand beside the bed is large enough to hold a lamp and has a drawer to store personal essentials. An armoire is out-fitted with shelves to hold clothing. Suitcases on top of the armoire store out of season items. The piece of furniture on the left is a piece that was designed to be used in a country dining room, but it works great in this bedroom. The drawers provide ample room for clothes storage and the shelves can hold books, cosmetics, a jewelry box, etc.

project

HOW TO CONVERT AN ARMOIRE

Traditionally, armoires were used to house hanging clothing because many bedrooms did not have closets. Today, newer homes have large closets so that armoires are not necessary for hanging clothes. However, armoires that have been retrofitted with shelves are very handy to have. Shelves can hold folded clothing, boxes of shoes, handbags, a television or stereo equipment, bed linens, towels, or extra blankets and pillows. This armoire is in a guest bedroom and holds linens for the bed in that room and extra towels for the guest bathroom. They look great in a room and are very versatile.

If the front of your armoire is not particularly pretty, or you want to cover a damaged part of the front, you can dress it up by placing full length mirrors on the doors. They add light and the illusion of space. Have the mirror panels cut to size. Use decorative molding to frame the mirror panels and hold them in place.

Two Ways to Add Shelves:

1. Measure and cut shelves to sizes needed. Cut small wooden blocks that are at least 3/4" wide to use as braces. Cut four to go under each shelf. Measure and mark armoire for placement of braces so that each is at the same height. Screw in place. Insert shelf to rest on brace.

2. When the armoire sides are too thin for attaching the brace with screws, glue the wooden braces to the armoire sides using heavy-duty wood glue. Allow to dry overnight before resting shelves on braces.

Covering Inside Doors:

The inside of the doors can be made more attractive by covering them with fabric panels. The panel shown has a criss-cross of ribbons that can be used to hold lightweight items such as old post cards, notes, etc.

1. Measure the panel area you wish to cover. Cut a piece of foam core board to this size.
2. Cut a piece of sheet batting to the same size. Place batting on top of foam core panel and add dots of glue in a few places to hold it lightly in place.
3. Cut a piece of fabric that is 4" longer and wider than panel measurement.
4. If you wish to add a criss-cross of ribbons, cut the number needed, cutting them to the same width of the fabric. It is best to trial-cut pieces of string or old ribbon to the sizes needed and place them to see if they will work or if they suit your needs. Then when you are sure you have the measurement and placement correct, you can cut your good pieces of ribbon. Sew ribbon to sides of the fabric with a few stitches. Sew a button to the fabric, attaching ribbon where the pieces cross.
5. Place the fabric panel face-down. Place the foam core panel onto the back of the fabric panel, with batting facing fabric. Pull fabric margins to the backside of foam core board and either glue or tape them to the back of the foam core panel.
6. Attach the panel by either gluing onto panel, attaching to panel with molding, or lightly tacking panel to door with small nails or tacks.

CLOTHES CLOSETS

If your closet is full of stuff you're not wearing, you're not alone. Did you know most women only wear 20% of what's in their closets? It's time to free yourself from closet clutter and have an organized, simplified wardrobe. Here are four good reasons:

Reason #1 – **Less is better.** Fewer clothes means having more to wear (believe it or not). If you only have ten outfits, but you look and feel great in all of them, you'll greet the day with anticipation instead of trying on three or four versions of a look you don't like, settling on one that's "not so bad," and heading off to work.

Reason #2 – **Circumstances change.** We tell ourselves the same stories. "Someday I'll have an occasion to wear that dress again." "Someday I'll lose weight and fit into those jeans." The truth is, if you do lose those ten pounds, you'll want to celebrate by buying a new pair of stylish jeans – you won't wear those old ones again.

Reason #3 – **Feeling good is important.** Look at each outfit and ask yourself, "How would this combination make me feel?" Or "How did I feel the last time I wore these pants? This shirt?" If the emotion isn't entirely positive, let the item go.

Reason #4 – **Life is short.** Life is too short let your bad shopping decisions claim your attention another day. Move on – to a closet with space to house your new positive, organized style.

Closet Guidelines

Okay, you're ready to clear out your closet. Here are some guidelines on what to keep:

- Keep clothes that pass the five-question test. (See "Clean Out Your Closet in 15 Minutes" for details.)

- Keep items you consider timeless classics. My classics list includes shirts that fit, cashmere sweaters, and suit parts. (I would, for example, keep the great pair of slacks and toss the jacket if it doesn't fit. Or hang onto a classic jacket and

15-minute

CLEAN OUT YOUR CLOSET

Make each piece of clothing pass this five-question test. If you can answer "yes" to every question, the item is a keeper. If you can't do the deed alone, ask a friend to help – someone with good taste and a loving laugh. Note: If it's been a long time since you cleaned out your closet, it may take more than 15 minutes. One option is to spend 15 minutes a day until the job is finished. Or, if you're working with a friend, spend part of a day (or the whole day, if that's what's necessary) and take a break every so often.

1. Does it fit? (Be honest! If you're not sure, try it on.)
2. Have you worn it recently? (If you can't remember, or if it was over a year ago, it's probably time to let it go.)
3. Is it in good condition? (If it shows signs of wear or is stained, it may be time to toss it.)
4. Do you love it? (You're not just keeping it because it has a designer label, are you? Does the fabric drape well? Is it a good color for you?)
5. Do you feel good about yourself when you wear it? (In other words, would you want to run into people you know when you're wearing it?)

Invest in quality hangers – no more wire hangers. Be ruthless. If an item doesn't pass the five-question test, give it away. ❏

Now that you've gotten rid of your closet clutter, use these tips for organizing your wonderful, wearable wardrobe.

- Sort clothes by groups, then by colors. If you want to wear a white shirt with your black slacks, you can see all your white shirt options at a glance. Sorting by groups and colors also makes it easy to see what items are missing – the things to add or replace the next time you shop.

- Arrange your clothing with the lightest colors in the back or in the darkest area of the closet. Your closet will look bigger and feel more spacious. It will also be easier to see what's in there.

- Store out-of-season clothes in large plastic containers. Drill small holes on the sides to allow for ventilation. Fabrics stored in plastic containers can't breathe, so invisible stains will darken in them. Inspect clothes under bright lights, checking for stains before storing them away. Do not use mothballs. The smell can stick around even after ten washings. Store these containers in your attic or under the bed. When you are ready to wear them again, refresh cotton and other washable items by placing them in the dryer with a damp towel for a ten-minute tumble. Steam wool items to release wrinkles.

let go of too-short pants.) Your list might include an Irish wool cardigan or a vintage kimono.

- Keep your keepsakes. Removing something from your closet doesn't mean you have to throw it out. If it's the pink sweater set you wore on your first date with your husband, by all means, save it – but store it somewhere else! Place it in an acid-free storage box with a label and put it in the attic, under the bed, or on the top shelf in your closet. It will always be there if you feel the need to visit it, and it won't get in the way of what you're going to wear tomorrow.

After the Clean-Out

Cleaning out your closet will also make you aware of what clothing items you don't have and (may) need. But don't rush out in a shopping frenzy. Be very selective about what you allow to join the elite, organized clothing collection that is now your wardrobe. Ask yourself those same five questions about any new acquisition. It had better be worthy.

HOW TO STORE VINTAGE CLOTHING & LINENS

Before you store any item, make sure it is clean. Food stains, body odor, or skin oils will permanently damage fabrics so it's important to take the time to launder the piece or spend the money to have it dry cleaned. Err on the side of caution – traces of substances like white wine may not be visible now, but they'll become visible over time.

If a garment or other textile looks (and is) clean, but smells musty or smoky, a good way to freshen it is simply to use a clothing steamer. **Do not** use products like odor-removal sprays on old textiles. If you must iron an old textile, iron on the wrong side of the cloth, on the lowest setting, and preferable with a clean white dish towel in between the iron and the garment as a pressing cloth.

Washing

Before washing an item, make sure the fabric is washable and that the colors won't run. To do this, find a small inconspicuous spot and test it with water and a little of your cleaning agent. Cotton and linen are usually safe to wash. Wool, silk, and blends usually are not. Some rayons are washable but may shrink.

Here's How:

1. Use your sink for small pieces and a bathtub for larger ones. Line the sink with a white pillowcase. Line a bathtub with a white sheet.
2. Fill the basin with lukewarm water and your cleaning agent. The Smithsonian Institution recommends clear glycerin face soap. Dissolve about 1/8 of a 3.5 oz. bar into the water. Never use detergents, even those intended for washing woolens or marketed as "gentle" – they are too harsh for old fabrics.
3. Place the item in the water and gently swish to agitate. Do not twist or wring the fabric. Allow the item to soak for at least 20 minutes, but not longer than 30 minutes. (If soaked too long, the fabric will reabsorb the dirt.)
4. Drain the water from the basin as you carefully lift two sides of the pillowcase or sheet away from the drain. This supports the fabric and protects it. (Remember that wet fabric is heavy and easily torn.)
5. Place the wet item on a dry white towel. Fold the towel over it and gently press the water from the piece. Don't wring or twist. Dry flat, either on a fresh towel or a mesh rack. *Option:* You can place it outside out of direct sunlight to dry.

Dry Cleaning

Dry cleaning can be risky. Make sure the cleaner has experience with old textiles, or check with a local museum for a recommendation. After cleaning, remove the item from the cleaner's plastic bag and allow the item to air out.

Storage

- **Fold everything.** *Never* hang antique or vintage clothing on hangers. It is best to fold everything. Try to limit the number of folds, and pad every fold with acid-free tissue paper.

- **Use a box.** Use archival, acid-free boxes for really special items such as genuine antiques and your wedding gown. You can purchase these boxes from archival supply companies and some dry cleaners. (Check the telephone directory or the Internet for sources.) A more affordable option is to line a cardboard box with acid-free tissue paper. If you are putting multiple items in one box, place the heaviest and largest items on the bottom and the lighter weight ones on top. Put acid-free paper between each item.

- **Never store fabrics in plastic.** Fabric has to breathe in order to stay mold- and mildew-free.

JEWELRY

Take the time to gather all your jewelry together and spread it out somewhere like your bed or dining room table where you can see all of it, and look through your collection.

If there are pieces you're no longer wearing, ask yourself why. Is the piece no longer "you" – is it too formal? too casual? too youthful? not stylish? Was it a gift now associated with an unpleasant memory? Is there a daughter, niece, or friend who might enjoy it more and wear it more often than you do? Pass it on! Or consider selling it.

As you peruse your collection, you may find treasures you'd forgotten. Look for new combinations – an old ring that would look great with your new bracelet, a turquoise-and-silver necklace that just matches your new cashmere sweater, three strands of beads that would be smashing worn all together with a simple dress.

Then move on to storing those items you want to keep and wear. Consider these organizing strategies:

Pictured right: One storage option is a multi-tier freestanding jewelry box.

Picutred below: Or use a drawer in a dresser or bathroom cabinet that's been fitted with trays and dividers.

- **Keep it in sight.** If you can't see and easily access your jewelry, the chances are good you're not wearing it. Designate a box or drawer in a convenient place so you can wear and enjoy your treasures, something with dividers that keep jewelry visible and untangled.

- **Have everything ready to wear.** If pearls or beads need restringing, get it done. Have clasps repaired. Get a new band for your watch before the old one breaks. Use tarnish-free trays for storing silver jewelry so it will maintain its polished appearance.

Continued on next page

79

Jewelry, continued

- **Organize by Color:** It is easy to find the right piece to wear when you have it all organized by color. Each drawer or tray should contain a single color type.

- **Organize by Type:** Place all your bracelets together, all rings, all necklaces. That sounds like a "no-brainer:" but when I started my organization of jewelry, I found that bracelets, earrings, and necklaces were all mixed together in one box.

- **Rotate your stock.** Like clothing, some jewelry may be seasonal. For example, if your heavy gold chain necklace looks out of place and feels hot and stuffy with summer linens, put it away for the season. If you know you won't be wearing those long, dangling earrings in the winter because they get caught on your knitted muffler and pull on your ears when you're driving your car, you know you won't be wearing them when it's cold. Store part of your collection.

- **Store keepsakes.** If you're holding onto a valuable heirloom until the right time comes to pass it along, put it in your safety deposit box. If there are items you know you'll never wear again but that you want to keep, store them somewhere else, away from the jewelry you're wearing. You can visit them when you want to, but they won't be taking up space among items you actually use and wear.

SHOE STORAGE SYSTEM

If you use this system, I guarantee you will wear all your shoes more often and enjoy the experience.

1. Store shoes in the boxes they came in or purchase a clear plastic shoe box for each pair.
2. Take a photo of each pair. (Be sure to show the heel height.) Tape the photo on the end of the box.
3. Stack the boxes on shelves or the floor of your closet. Store shoes on shelves based on how often you wear them. Black silk evening shoes (for most of us) belong on the very top shelf. (A handy stepstool will let you reach them.) Athletic shoes you wear every day – no box, lower shelf.
4. Store out of season shoes in plastic containers that you can move to the attic or place under the bed. Place a clothes dryer sheet in the container to eliminate odors.

Pictured right: Having photos of your shoes allows you to see all your shoe options at a glance.

READING MATERIAL

Magazines, books, and catalogues can pile up fast if you don't sort and purge from time to time. I keep a large round basket under my bedside table and use it to hold reading materials. Every few weeks, I sort out the basket – keepers (things I haven't read yet) go back in the basket, catalogues I've perused go to the recycle bin, and magazines and books I'm finished with but not planning to keep get placed in a shopping bag. After checking other reading spots throughout the house (other bedrooms, bathrooms, and the home office) and separating the good from the read, I put the bag in my car. When I'm out, I drop it off at a charity waiting room, hospital, clinic, or senior center. With this system, instead of dreading this organizing project, I actually look forward to it because I know someone else is going to enjoy reading a great book or magazine I've enjoyed.

Begin every organizing project by reducing the amount of stuff you have.

TELEVISION & MUSIC IN THE BEDROOM

If you watch TV in bed or like to listen to great music before you drift off to sleep, organize accordingly and create an entertainment unit for your bedroom. There are options for every budget.

If you can afford one and have the space, get a cabinet-type entertainment center. Or buy a rolling cart-type unit for your TV and other electronic equipment. (Don't put the TV on top of your dresser.)

Or perhaps you have an old armoire, storage cabinet, or bookcase that you can use? Start by taking measurements and assessing your storage needs. You may need to rearrange or add shelves, remove the back, or cut holes to accommodate electrical cords and cables or the depth of the television. Paint to match your decor, and staple fabric over the back if you had to remove or cut holes in the wooden back. (You can put the cabinet in a corner so the back won't show.)

UNDER-BED STORAGE

Make use of the space under your bed – don't let it be a haven for lost shoes and dust bunnies. Solutions designed specifically for under-bed storage are available, including drawers, plastic and cardboard storage boxes, and fabric and plastic-covered frames with zippers. They're great for out-of-season items, bed linens, blankets, or memorabilia. If your bed is too low to accommodate an under-the-bed box, you can purchase risers that are made especially for raising a bed.

Pictured below: A plastic under-bed storage box on wheels. Purchased risers are used to raise the bed so there is room for the box.

ORGANIZING KIDS' BEDROOMS

Many children's bedrooms are too small and have way too little storage space, but the reason most children don't keep their rooms tidy is that they don't have homes for their stuff. They need help from you in the form of guidance and storage solutions.

I have always been fascinated by the differences among children that all grew up in the same family with the same parents in the same environment. My two children, a son and a daughter, couldn't be more different. One is a neat freak, while the other – well, let's just say the other is a work in process. You may have the same mix of styles in your family. If you do, learn to embrace these differences and help them get organized and stay that way by developing systems and creating homes for all of their stuff.

15-minute

SORTING STRATEGY FOR KIDS

GATHER:

Your child

A patient attitude

4 large empty bins or boxes

GO:

Working with the child, pick up and sort items into these four bins:

• **Keeper Bin**

Items that are worn often or played with at least once a week go into this bin. Children's clothes are easy to sort and dispose of because they outgrow them so quickly. Be harsh; if there is any doubt, don't put it into this bin. Place out-of-season clothes in a separate stack to be sorted later.

• **Throwaway Bin**

Place any item that is stained, torn, or damaged in this bin. Add any broken toys, incomplete games, or unwanted artwork or craft items in here, too. Charities don't want your kids' broken or damaged items any more than you do.

• **Hand-Me-Down Bin**

If you have a large family and pass clothing and outgrown toys down the line to younger siblings (or cousins) or have friends with children younger than yours, put outgrown keepers in this bin. But be specific, and don't keep anything that won't be used. Ask yourself if your younger daughter will really wear that hot pink t-shirt. (Is she the more conservative type who only wears button-downs?) Does your younger son love model airplanes or dinosaurs like the older one or is he interested only in sports?

• **Charity Bin**

Any good, undamaged item that doesn't have a current user at your household needs to go into this bin. Don't wait for the bin to get full. When you have finished your 15-minute sorting task go ahead and put it in the car, and the next time you are out drop it off. (And remember to get a tax receipt.)

Kids can't keep their rooms tidy if they don't have homes for their stuff.

Storage Solutions for Kids' Rooms

- **Crate it.** Colorful, stackable plastic or wooden crates are a good solution. You can line the walls with them and use them to store clothes, toys, and school supplies.

- **Add shelves.** Consider installing wire shelving inside closets. Most children's clothes are easier to store folded than hung. Extra shelving installed within reach will make it easier for them to assist with cleanup and help keep their rooms organized. Use higher shelves for out-of-season clothes.

- **Keep it open.** Open containers like baskets, bins, or plastic dishpans can contain toys, games, sports equipment, and craft items. Since they are easier for kids to access than containers with lids, they are more apt to be put to use.

- **Put it under the bed.** Underbed storage is a great solution. You can purchase risers for older children's beds that provide a few extra valuable inches of storage space under the bed. Fill inexpensive plastic crates or underbed boxes with toys or out-of-season items and store them under the bed.

- **Let's roll.** If drawers are overstuffed, try rolling t-shirts and other clothing items instead of storing them flat. If they are folded smoothly before rolling they won't get as wrinkled, and more items are visible when the drawer is open. If you use storage crates, you can also use them to store rolled items (jeans, sweats, pajamas) "on end" – they'll be readily visible. Rolling also makes it easy to pack for weekend trips or family vacations. The rolled clothes go quickly from the crate or drawer right into the suitcase.

Storing Games & Puzzles

Games and puzzles are not items most families use every-day, but it's important to designate storage spots for them so you can find them when you want them. To make a plan, gather your games, survey your collection, and assess your storage needs.

If at all possible keep games and puzzles in their original boxes. (You can do a little repair work with clear package tape, if necessary, to make the boxes last longer.) Tape an envelope inside the lid of the box to store the instructions if they are not printed on the box. Use small clear plastic stack-able containers to store loose game pieces, decks of cards, poker chips, and score pads and pencils.

Clear plastic storage tubs with handles work well for hold-ing game and puzzle boxes. You can store them by type or by intended age group (all games and puzzles for kids 5 and under, for 5- to 12-year-olds, for teenagers and adults.) Put them in the appropriate storage tub and label the container with a complete list of its contents. The tubs can be stored on a shelf in the garage, on a high closet shelf (for the older crowd), or on the floor of a closet (for the younger set).

When it's time for a game, the tub comes out. After play-time is over, the game gets packed back into its box, put back in the tub, and stored away.

Above: A plastic dishpan holds doll-size dishes, making it easy to set the table for a tea party and clean up when it's over.

Pictured left: Colorful plastic containers contain and organize books and toys on shelves.

Pictured opposite page: Paint and fabric can turn a dilapidated piece of furniture into a one-of-a-kind treasure. On this armoire, the door with the gathered curtain displays a little girl's jewelry; a fabric-covered panel installed in the other door has criss-crossed satin rib-bons to hold photos and memorabilia. The drawer on the bottom is within easy reach of a child.

CHAPTER 7

Organizing
YOUR
Bathroom

The bathroom is such a personal space – we all have our own needs and little quirks. Because we're typically in there early in the morning as we get ready to greet the outside world and late in the evening when we're winding down from the day, we need bathrooms that are energizing *and* relaxing. Having an organized bathroom helps achieve both goals.

STRATEGY

- Provide storage solutions for the everyday items used by the folks who share the space.

- Supply a place to hang clothes while getting dressed or bathing. Example: Attach hooks on the back of the bathroom door for robes and pajamas.

- Accept a new attitude about the products you don't use and makeup you never wear.

- If there are kids in your house (or clumsy adults), use plastic – not glass – containers for all your bath storage needs.

- Be Safe! Put medicines, first aid supplies, and extra razors in a clear plastic shoebox with a secure lid. Store it on a high shelf in the linen closet or in an upper cabinet in your kitchen. It doesn't have to be in the bathroom, but family members should be aware of where it is. Tape a note to the top of the box with the poison control center emergency number, 911, and other important phone numbers plus your address and phone number. This keeps you from having to think during a real family emergency.

Don't buy more than you can store.

Cleaning Supplies

Keep bathroom cleaning supplies in a plastic tote or bucket, which will keep chemicals from leaking or spilling onto shelves and damaging expensive cabinets. The tote or bucket also makes carrying products around the bath easy and safe. If you have small children, store cleaning products safely on higher shelves out of the reach of little ones or in a cabinet with a safety latch.

Pictured left: Fill a painted tin bucket with unwrapped rolls of toilet paper. Everyone will be able to find them, and it will be easy to see when your supply is running low.

Pictured left: If your bathroom has lots of base cabinets, optimize the storage space and put everything within easy reach by installing pullout shelves behind the cabinet doors. For how-to information, see the section, "Organizing Your Kitchen."

15-minute
MEDICINE CABINET CLEANUP

To organize your medicine cabinet, you have to let go and be willing to do a little sorting and grouping. If things don't fall out of your medicine cabinet every time you reach for an item, you can skip this project and move on to towels. But before you do, give yourself a star because you must be the only disorganized person in the world with a clean, easy-to-use medicine cabinet!

GATHER:
Plastic container or shoe box
Cleaning supplies
Small see-through containers
Paper and pen or pencil

GO:
1. **Analyze.** Analyze the space you have to work with and decide which items you need to store and easily retrieve daily or weekly.

2. **Eliminate.** Let go of all expired items, be they medicines, makeup, or personal care products. Out they go! Then pitch the items that you never use, any empty containers, and items with tattered packaging. (If the package is tattered, it's probably time to replace that item.) Make a list of items you need to replace.

3. **Sort.** Remove everything you don't use at least once a week. Place those items in a plastic container or small shoebox. They can be stored in a drawer or another cabinet. What's left are the items that you should store in your medicine cabinet. (Everyone's list is different.)

4. **Clean.** Take everything out of your medicine cabinet and clean it thoroughly.

5. **Rearrange.** Group your items by height rather than product type. If your shelves are adjustable, rearrange them to accommodate the various height groupings. Turn the products so the labels face forward for easy identification. Use small see-through containers to organize small items (hair accessories, clippers, twisters, brushes). Small glasses or cups work well. ❑

TOWELS

Every bath needs space for keeping towels of various sizes and washcloths. Storing them can be both decorative and functional.

Pictured right: An old painted chair provides a touch of color and a place to stack towels and a bar of soap for a guest.

Pictured below: Clean rolled-up hand towels are within easy reach when kept in a wall-hung basket.

Towel Storage Options

- To maximize storage space, roll your towels and put them in a basket.

- Roll wash cloths and place them on a decorative tray or platter.

- Keep hand towels and washcloths organized and within easy reach in an antique bowl (it doesn't have to be a perfect one). If you don't have counter space, set it atop a small bench, stool, or table.

- If cabinet space is limited but you have room for a chair, fold your towels and stack them on it. You can find fabulous single chairs at reasonable prices at thrift stores and yard sales.

- Hang your towels on a towel ladder. Use a vintage wooden ladder or turn the page to see how to make one.

project

MAKING A TOWEL LADDER

Colorful, plushy towels look wonderful displayed on a towel ladder. This one is easy to make, and it's assembled without hardware. You can cut all the lumber yourself or have the 1x4s and 1" dowels cut to the proper lengths at the store.

YOU'LL NEED:

2 pine 1x4s, each 56" long

4 dowels, 1" diameter, each 17" long

8 dowels, 1/4" diameter, each 1-1/2" long

Drill and 1" and 1/4" drill bits

Hand saw

Measuring tape

Pencil

Sandpaper

Rag

Rubber mallet

HERE'S HOW:

1. Measure and mark the placement for the rungs in the center of the 1x4s, starting 4" from the end of one 1x4 and placing three more marks 12" apart. (Fig. 1) Repeat to mark the other 1x4.

2. Using a 1" drill bit, drill holes at the marks.

3. Measure and mark each 1" dowel 2" from each end. Switch to the 1/4" drill bit and drill holes through the 1" dowels at the marked holes.

4. Lightly sand all the wood to smooth the drilled holes, the cut ends, and any rough spots. Wipe away the sanding dust.

5. Working on the floor, lay the 1x4s parallel to each other, lining up the drilled holes. Slip the 1" dowels through the holes to create the ladder, positioning the ends of the dowels so they protrude on each end with the drilled holes on the outside. (The side members will be 12" apart.) Use a rubber mallet to help position the dowels, as needed.

6. Slip the 1/4" dowels through the drilled holes to hold the rungs in place. (See the photo.) ❑

The 1/4" dowel holds the 1" dowel in place without nails or screws.

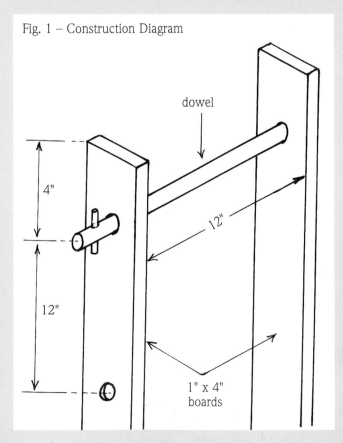

Fig. 1 – Construction Diagram

dowel

4"

12"

12"

1" x 4" boards

SPA STUFF

There are lots of options for containing and organizing bath essentials and luxuries in and around the tub or shower. You're more likely to use and enjoy items like bath salts and shower gel when they are close at hand and you don't have to hunt for them when you're ready for a relaxing soak or a reviving shower.

- **Display on the counter.** If counter space allows, use decorative glass or plastic canisters to store cotton swabs, cotton balls, bath salts, bubble bath, etc. Crocks, vases, or taller glasses provide accessible storage for makeup brushes, combs, and pencil liners.

- **Put them on a tray.** Use a wire bath tray to hold shampoo, sponges, scrubbies, razor, bath gel, and other items you use each time you bathe. When you clean the tub, it is easy to lift the tray out of your way and easy to access everything you need when you're in the tub.

- **Shelve them.** In the shower choose a sturdy plastic-coated wire or stainless steel storage unit with open shelves that hooks over the showerhead. Use it to hold soap, razor, and bottles of shampoo and body wash, freeing up the shower floor, the edge of the tub, or valuable medicine cabinet or countertop storage space. (It's easy to clean, too.)

- **Hang 'em up.** Add hooks in the shower stall or above the tub to hold body brushes, wet washcloths, hand washables, and dripping swimsuits in the summer. Use suction cups to hold lightweight brushes, scrub mitts, and a squeegee.

- **Use baskets.** Use a basket to organize beauty supplies, hair dryer, brushes, and hair accessories, and set it on an antique wooden chair or a stool next to the tub. Hang a basket near the tub to organize spa supplies for easy access and an attractive display.

- **Bag them.** Store bath-time toys (or any bath essentials you might move from bathroom to bathroom) in a nylon mesh bag and hang it from the faucet to drain and dry. It's easy to remove when guests need to share the kids' bathroom, and since items in a mesh bag can dry thoroughly, it also stops mildew.

Pictured left: Under-sink cabinets are rarely fitted with shelves, but there's a lot of space down there to use. One solution is slide-out plastic drawers, which can be stacked to fill the space and used to organize and stow makeup, first aid supplies, and hair dryers and accessories – whatever you need to store. Their solid tops also can be used as shelves for items like boxes of tissues. Wire baskets on sliding rails are another option.

MAKEUP

Organizing your makeup is a two-step process. First, reduce your supply; then, rearrange what's left. You'll be amazed at how much easier it is to get ready.

Makeup and other beauty products have a limited shelf life. Anything more than a year old (six months is really more realistic) should be thrown out. This simple strategy will reduce the amount of storage space you need for beauty products.

After that, throw out makeup you're not using, like those tubes of hot pink lipstick that were a free gift from your favorite cosmetics company. We don't need six bottles of foundation or a dozen eye shadows – most of us use only one or two colors of lipstick, eye shadow, blush, etc. Now is the time to pitch them. If you can't bring yourself to part with that never-used tube of lipstick or whatever, try this simple test: Wear it today. If, by the end of the day, you are happy with it, keep it. If not – well, you know the answer: Throw it out.

When you're ready to rearrange, here are some strategies:

- Use drawer dividers custom fit to your drawers to store your everyday makeup and beauty products.
- If drawer space is limited, use a basket for makeup that can be slid on a shelf or under the sink.
- Use clear plastic makeup bags to store manicure supplies and makeup.
- Even simpler, place a small basket on the vanity for easy access and quick pick-up.

Organized for Travel

If you travel frequently, consider buying two of each of your everyday makeup and bath products and keeping one set in large clear zipper-top plastic bags. You can quickly toss

the bags in your luggage for a last-minute trip – you'll never again arrive at your destination without your mascara or favorite lipstick.

The plastic bags also make for quick unpacking. When you reach your destination, set out your plastic bags of makeup, hair products, and spa supplies on the bathroom counter and in the shower. When it's time to leave, re-seal the bags, pack them in your luggage, and off you go. Rotate the products with your day-to-day supply if you find you don't use them up in six months.

Pictured above: A drawer with dividers holds makeup and grooming products. Tip: Choose black dividers – makeup will stain white or light-colored ones.

CHAPTER 8

Organizing
YOUR
Crafts Room

It's much easier to satisfy your creative impulses when your supplies and tools are organized. This section includes ideas for organizing photos and memorabilia, gift wrap, cards, sewing supplies, and art supplies like paint brushes, markers, and colored pencils.

Pictured opposite page: Don't overlook the benefits of using your pitchers or vases as storage containers. Using these great shapes to organize your supplies frees up storage space while you enjoy the color and texture they add to your rooms.

STRATEGY

- Enjoy the view. Being able to see your tools and supplies can spark the creative impulse. Keep supplies for projects at hand so they are easy to find and use.

- Make creative use of containers for organizing tools and supplies.

- Arrange according to the space available. Your "crafts room" may be a studio, an armoire, a closet, or spaces in several rooms in your house. The laundry room can be the perfect place for crafts and flower arranging, for example, especially if you have a sink and you have the space.

Pictured right: An armoire fitted with shelves can make any room (family room, guest room, dining room) a crafts room or home office. Boxes can hold supplies or important papers. There's ample room for reading material, reference books, and notebooks for journaling or jotting down ideas.

Satisfying creative impulses is much easier when

PHOTOS & MEMORABILIA

Few things are more troublesome than dealing with piles of unmarked, undated photos, disorganized negatives, and photo CDs jammed into drawers and boxes throughout the house. Here are some tips to help you preserve cherished memories. Years later, you will be happy you took the time to protect your valuable photo history.

Getting everything into one location is key. To do this, gather two cardboard storage boxes. Visit every drawer in your home and look for photos, negatives, and other keepsakes like children's drawings, Mother's Day cards, and special notes you've kept over the years. Place all the photo-related items in one box and the memorabilia in the other.

If you have a lot of photo items to organize, start by dividing them into three simple stacks: Photos (prints), negatives, and photo CDs or other digital media. Then sort the photos into stacks by subject (his family, my family, kids, friends, vacations, houses, holidays) or date (the year, specific holidays, seasons of the year, historic or vintage photos). If you are lucky enough to still have the negatives with the photos – great! Label them with the subject and date or the event where they were taken before you separate them. (But don't get bogged down in this walk down memory lane.)

Now that you can see what you need to store, you can assess the type, size, and number of storage containers you need to organize your important collection. Shop for containers, being sure to select products that are photo friendly and labeled acid free and/or lignin free and PVC free. Lignin is a natural by-product of wood processing that can damage photos. Photo albums with PVC (polyvinyl chloride) plastic sleeves can harm photos. If you have stored photos in these types of albums, remove them now and put them in photo-safe albums or storage boxes.

When you've assembled your boxes and albums, fill them with photos, label them, and put them away. This is a great time to select a few favorite photos and put them into frames so you can enjoy them all over again. I like to file my photos by holidays and display them in seasonal frames to decorate for that particular holiday.

Use the same sorting strategy for cards, letters, and memorabilia (by subject or by date).

Pictured left: Photo boxes are affordable and attractive. They come in a huge variety of colors and designs and have label holders attached.

supplies and tools are organized.

Where to Store Memorabilia

Heat, moisture, sunlight, and dust are the enemies of photos and negatives – just handling photos over and over can damage them. It's best to store photos in a dry, dark, cool place – never the attic, basement, or garage. The same goes for cards and other paper memories – they, too, can be damaged by dampness and hot temperatures. Upper shelves of closets are ideal for storing photos and smaller paper items. That way, they are out of the way of everyday traffic and make good use of shelves too tall for convenient daily access.

For your children's drawings and school papers, purchase under-the-bed plastic storage containers. Slide them under the bed or stack them on high closet shelves. Label each box with the year and/or the child's name.

GIFT WRAPPING SUPPLIES

If you enjoy creating beautifully wrapped packages and rolls of ribbon inspire you, you'll need a place to keep your stash of supplies.

- **All together, out of sight.** Use a large wicker laundry hamper, one large enough to stand rolls of wrapping paper on end. Purchase 1/2" diameter wooden dowels to hold rolls of ribbon. Secure a heavy cardboard disc to one end, then slip the rolls of ribbon on the dowel and stand it inside the hamper. Hang gift bags from the side of the hamper on S-hooks. Fill one large bag with gift tags, tape, scissors, and a pen and add it to the hamper. Keep it inside a closet and bring it out when you need to use it.

- **All together, out in the open.** Find a decorative wooden "tool box." Use one side for rolls of ribbon, the other for folded and rolled wrapping papers and cards. Display it on a shelf or on top of a cabinet. Carry it to a counter or table for use.

- **Divided and displayed.** Use baskets or boxes you can display on a tabletop or hang on the wall to artfully display rolls of ribbons, cards, and gift bags. Or hang rolls of ribbon from a rod. Put rolls of paper in a tall wire or wicker basket. Enjoy their beautiful colors and shapes.

Pictured above: Hang a decorative curtain rod on the wall with brackets and use it to store rolls of ribbon. Tie a piece of elastic to one handle of a scissors and loop the other end over the rod. When you want to cut a length of ribbon, you won't have to hunt for the scissors.

Picutred above: A basket of gift wrapping supplies can be an artful display.

Pictured below: A decorative tool box filled with wrapping supplies can be carried to table or counter.

DECORATING IDEAS

Keep track of interior design projects and ideas in colorful, matching file folders and display them in a color-coordinated file box on your desk. Use a marker in a coordinating color to label them. Use transparent plastic boxes with securely latched tops for storing samples of carpeting and fabrics.

PENCILS & PENS

Displaying art supplies like colored pencils and markers in transparent canisters allows easy access and the added benefits of being able to enjoy and be inspired by the array of colors.

Magazine Sorting Tips

If you subscribe to or purchase lots of decorating, food, gardening, or lifestyle magazines, chances are there are articles and photos you want to keep for inspiration or future reference. If you do, you'll need a system for organizing them so that when you want to locate them, you'll know just where and how to look. Here are some organizing options:

Option #1 – Sort by Season
Sort magazines you want to keep by season, not title. When you get ready to plan Thanksgiving dinner, you can locate all the October and November issues and find everything from recipes to fall flower arrangements.

Option #2 – Follow the Five-Year Rule
Keep all the issues of favorite magazines in chronological order, but no longer than five years. Why? After about five years, styles, products, and colors will have changed completely, and the ideas will be dated. Every year, add new ones and recycle the oldest issues.

Option #3 – Rip, Then Sort by Topic
Flip through your stack of magazines once they are two to three months old. Rip out ONLY the ideas you really like and think you would actually take the time and money to duplicate. Recycle the rest of the publication. Sort the pages into simple categories, such as "Gardening," "Decorating," "Recipes," and "Entertaining." Store them in folders in a filing cabinet or desktop file box.

Pictured above: Use labeled magazine storage boxes to hold magazines sorted by season.

Make a list of simple little organization projects

SEWING SUPPLIES

If you sew, you need a place to keep tools like your sewing machine, scissors, thread trimmers, pinking shears, a seam ripper, a bodkin, and a darning egg, plus supplies like chalk and spools of thread handy and ready to use. Having a room set up for sewing is ideal. Second best is space in an out-of-the-way location, like a guest room or den where you can have a desk or table set up and ready. But if that's not possible or realistic, a rolling cart or one of the new organizers on wheels that looks like a suitcase will allow you to set up your current project in no time at any location in the house. When you're finished, you simply pack up your machine and your tools in the organizer and roll it to a closet for storage.

Pictured right: The sewing closet. A suitcase-style rolling organizer holds a sewing machine and sewing tools and stores easily in a closet. Stacked clear plastic drawers can hold patterns, fabrics, and yarn. Briefcase-style plastic boxes with hinged lids contain pieces of current projects until completion. Storing multiple yards of fabric on rolls is a better option than folding. Tools for pattern drafting and measuring can be hung on the wall.

that would improve your day.

GREETING CARD STORAGE

Rather than having to shop for just the right card on a deadline, buy greeting cards when you come across ones you like in stores or assemble some supplies and make a few. Use a pretty file box with a hinged lid to organize them by occasion (birthday, retirement, new baby, housewarming, get well, sympathy, anniversary) and to hold boxes of thank you notes and blank cards. The box will keep them wrinkle-, dust-, and moisture-free.

CHAPTER 9

Organizing YOUR Home Office

Whether you are an entrepreneur working from home or just looking for a cozy little spot to surf the Internet, write a letter, or manage the family finances, every home needs an office. Your home office doesn't have to be a separate room, but you do need enough space to organize the stuff that keeps your family in sync with the outside world. Visiting and using a room you love makes any activity in that room more enjoyable and productive. Why not pay bills in an attractive, well-organized space instead of sitting on the floor, surrounded by chaos?

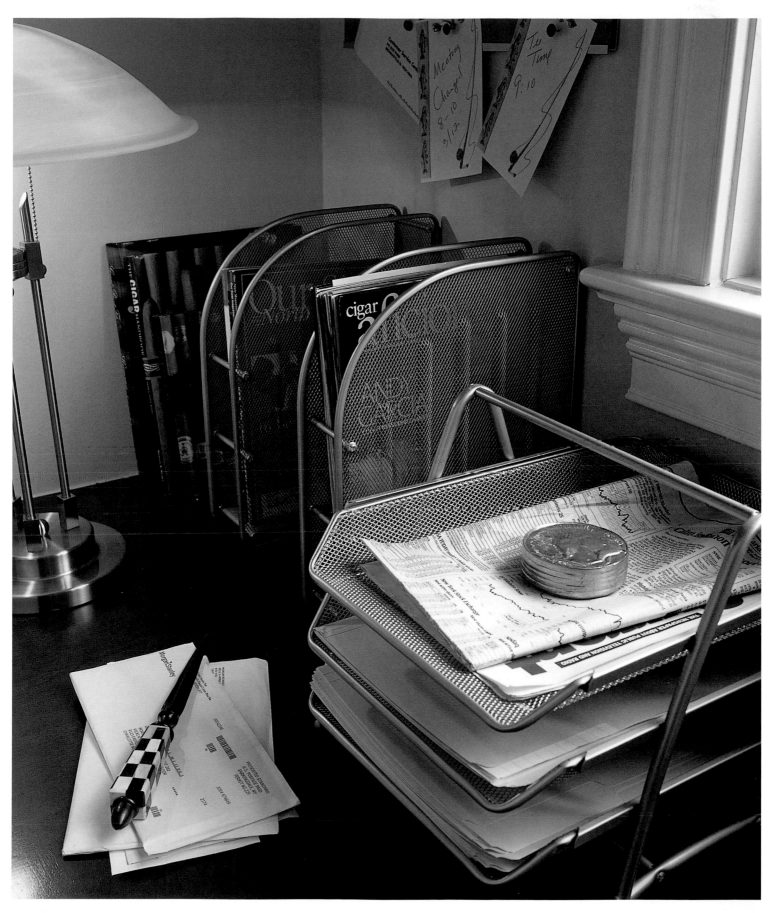

STRATEGY

- **Acknowledge technology.** Today's busy world demands that we plug into technology. Computers, printers, cell phones, lamps, and chargers all need a source of electricity and the equipment to protect them from power surges.

- **Choose a space.** You don't have to have a lot of space, but it needs to provide a measure of privacy and, most importantly, accessibility for everyone who needs to use it. Your home office might be a closet off the kitchen or a space at the end of a hallway. You might be able to create a great little niche in the family room for your communications area. Or purchase a computer hutch – it will look great in any room. You can open it up and work away, then close things up when it's time for company or entertaining.

- **Carve out a niche.** Under the stairs is a great option in some homes. Built-in cabinets or a table with a lamp and chair can provide just the space you need to get a handle on your home telecommunications and finances. You can even make a well-organized basket a portable home office. For the ultimate in flexibility, think about installing wireless Internet service at your house so your communications center/home office can be located anywhere – even in the garage or on the screened porch.

- **Keep it organized.** The more people sharing the area, the more everything needs a place.

- **Group supplies.** Things that are used together should be stored together. For example: keep stamps and address labels next to envelopes.

- **Choose useful, creative containers.** People are more inclined to keep themselves organized if the containers they use are creative, attractive, and user friendly. Pencil holders are a good example. People like them because they are easy to use and accessible. In your away-from-home-office, your pencil holder might be a stainless steel mesh cylinder or the promotional coffee cup a client gave you. But in your home office, you can surround yourself with the things you love, like pottery coffee cups, glassware, metal canisters, flowerpots, baskets, or paper-covered boxes.

- **Develop systems for handling your household business.** What you need depends on your family's activities and schedules. You might want to post a large calendar on the wall and encourage family members to note their appointments and events. Or have a bulletin board or folder to hold schedules for sports events, school holidays, or trash and recycling pickups – anything you need to keep track of.

- **Keep track of important papers.** Most of us are careless with our important papers. We forget where we stored them, but we know they're here somewhere. That's because our most important papers are ones we only need once in a great while, like passports, birth certificates, titles to cars, the deed to the house, and the warranty for the TV. It is easy to keep these papers organized if you simply put them in a container where they can be laid flat or organized in files and store the container away on a high shelf. For really important items, like wills, birth certificates, and life insurance policies, rent a safe deposit box at the bank. The rest of the stuff, we just need to sort, file, and forget unless the television breaks, we sell the car or the house, or we're planning a trip to Europe.

- **Always recycle and clear out the clutter.**

Pictured opposite page: This home office takes up one wall in the family room. This large free-standing furniture unit is used by the entire family. When the desk surface is not in use, it slides back into the furniture piece.

WORK SPACES

The key to creating a comfortable, inviting home office is finding just the right mix of high tech and cozy haven. Here are some ideas:

- Use small baskets or old wooden toolboxes as mail and bill sorters.

- Use wicker or twig baskets to hold files.

- Old trunks and chests can store tax returns, warranties, or school artwork. They also double as stands for printers and file baskets. For easy retrieval, make a list of items you have stored in the chest and keep it handy.

- Try old wire baskets as trash cans.

- Put a table lamp on your desk.

- Buy an electric pencil sharpener and sharpen all your pencils. (Don't you just hate how you keep picking up the same old pencil with the broken lead over and over? Pitch it or sharpen it.)

- Use large sea shells to hold paper clips, rubber bands, or push pins.

- Put your pencils in a small pitcher.

- Hang things on the wall. Install a bulletin board and use it as a message center. Hang a wall calendar to keep track of events and appointments. Use a wipe-off note board for jotting down phone numbers and reminders.

- Use a Rolodex-type card organizer to keep phone numbers handy. It's really easy to staple business cards from the plumber, baby sitter service, and the Chinese carryout to the cards. When you find a better plumber or a new babysitter moves into the neighborhood, pitch the old card and insert one with the new information.

Pictured right: This large free-standing unit has plenty of space for files and other supplies – yet takes up only a corner of a room. This would be a perfect piece for a family room, a guest room, or even in the bedroom.

CALENDARS

- Choose the calendar that works best for you. I like month by month calendars. Other people only want to see one day or a week at a time. If you are serious about being organized, think about getting a yearly wall calendar that you can write on and wipe off. It really lets you see what's ahead and keeps you from being so overwhelmed and disorganized the first few days of the new month.

- Keep only one calendar. Or two, one for your away-from-home office or business, and another for home and family. (But never more than two!)

- Jot down appointments on your calendar, not on sticky notes or small pieces of paper – you'll keep moving that note from spot to spot until it gets lost. Once it's on the calendar, pitch the note. Being organized means not having to handle the same items over and over while you are looking for something else.

quick project

MAKING IDENTIFICATION STICKERS

Sometimes when you share a home office, things don't always get put back in the same place each time. To avoid frustration, make stickers to be placed into each section of your organizer.

This is a great project that you can let the kids help with. Stickers are easy to make using your home computer. Simply type the name of the article, or find some clip art that illustrates the article. Print this on self-adhesive paper. Cut out the illustrations or words and stick to the organizer.

HANDLING YOUR BILLS & MAIL

Pictured above: A three-bin method for sorting mail: one for magazines, one for the rest of the mail you want to keep, and one for trash. Take the magazine bin to the place where you like to read, the mail you want to keep to the home office, and the paper trash to the recycle bin. Don't forget to shred those pre-approved credit card offers and any trash that contains personal information like account numbers.

Whether you use folders, baskets, or bins, it's important to sort and organize the mail every day as it arrives to eliminate pileups and having to sort through stacks of paper to find what you need when the time comes to pay a bill, respond to an invitation, or keep an appointment.

- **Sort your mail every day.** Pitch junk mail into a basket by your door for recycling. Divide the household mail into categories such as these three: bills to pay, invitations and personal correspondence, and "maybe." The maybe category includes interesting offers, charitable requests, catalogues, and flyers you are actually going to read and possibly use. (But do clear out the clutter – don't save a carpet-cleaning offer if you just had your rugs cleaned or you don't have rugs.)

- **Separate the bills from the rest of the mail.** If you do one thing, this is it. Kept in the stack with everything else, bills can get lost (so can an invitation to a great party another reason to sort). Move the bills and the invitations and correspondence to your home office.

- **Develop a bill-paying system.** Organize your bills based on the way you pay them, and create your own filing system based on your payment schedule. If you pay everything once a month, store them all together in a drawer, box, or folder. If you're on a weekly or daily system, check out a 31-day sorter. If you mail your bills, keep supplies you need for bill paying (stamps, address labels, stapler) together.

- **Use stand-up file holders** so you can access information quickly and put it away just as fast. Buy a pack of colorful file folders and label one for each recurring event – "School," "Church," "Basketball Team," "Book Group." After you've reviewed the mail, jot down important dates and times on your calendar and drop the information in the right folder. When it comes time for the event, you can easily find the community newsletter, permission slip, map, or invitation.

project

PAPER COVERED OFFICE
ORGANIZERS

Ordinary, inexpensive cardboard organizers like file folders and magazine holders from office supply and crafts stores can be transformed into attractive, color-coordinated desktop accessories. Simply cover them with decorative paper or fabric and embellish. Cover a series or set of organizers for a coordinated look. For a fun, coordinated look, use stickers and paper cutouts to decorate plain manila file folders.

continued on page 116

project

PAPER COVERED OFFICE ORGANIZERS

YOU'LL NEED:

A box
Decorative paper or fabric
White craft glue
Paint brush
Paper or fabric shears, for cutting the cover pieces
Small scissors, for cutting out motifs
Tweezers, for placing motifs
Measuring tape
Embellishments and trims, such as ribbons, metal label
   holders, charms

HERE'S HOW:

To Cover with Paper:

You can cover a box with a single sheet of paper if the paper you want to use is bigger than the dimensions of the

box. For larger boxes or to use smaller sheets of paper like calendar prints or pages from old books or magazines, overlap the paper pieces, gluing them in place one at a time.

To use a single sheet of paper:

1. Measure the container end to end and side to side. Add 2" to each dimension for overlap. Cut a piece of paper to size.
2. Wrap the piece of paper around the box, letting it overlap the top and bottom by 1". Fold to crease around the edges and bends, allowing the paper to overlap at one corner. Remove the paper.
3. Dilute glue with enough water so that it can be brushed on in a thin layer.
4. Using the overlapping edge as your starting point, brush glue on the overlapping paper and secure to the box. Then move to the adjacent side and brush glue on that side of the box. Press the paper against the box over the glue. Continue working, one side of the box at a time, applying glue and pressing the paper in place, until you reach the last side.

Here small flower motifs are cut out with decoupage scissors. Rather than trying to calculate spacing for centering motifs as you're covering containers, use a paper with an all-over design to cover the container, then add cutout motifs to decorate the space. Papers created especially for decoupage are good sources.

5. Check the fit on the last edge, trimming as necessary to fit flush on the corner where you began. Apply the glue and press the paper in place.
6. Turn the box on its side and glue the paper to the bottom, folding in and affixing the excess at the corners. Stand the box right side up. Fold the paper over the top edge and secure with glue, one side at a time. Let dry.
7. Decorate with paper cutouts, ribbons, and/or metal charms, securing them in place with glue. ❑

To cover with overlapping pieces:
1. Place the paper on the box, trying out the placement and creasing it around corners and edges. Trim the paper pieces as necessary. Remove the paper.
2. Dilute glue with enough water so that it can be brushed on in a thin layer.
3. Apply glue with a brush to the back of one piece of paper at a time and press it on the box. Repeat the process, using another sheet of paper, until the box is covered.
4. Decorate with paper cutouts, ribbons, and/or metal charms, securing them in place with glue. ❑

Top: Here, flower cluster cutouts are glued to strips of decorative paper. These strips will be used as borders to go along edges of notebooks or around cans or across fronts of boxes.

Center: Use metal label holders or charms to add three-dimensional decoration to covered containers. Here, floral motifs are cut out and positioned to flank a metal basket. The paper pieces are glued in place, then the basket is glued on top.

Bottom: Paper printed with script can also be a source of motifs – use some of the cutout words as fanciful labels for holders or folders. Embellish with cutouts of floral motifs or greenery.

117

quick projects

RIBBON LATTICE BULLETIN BOARD

Pictured on opposite page.

Use ribbon to create a lattice effect on a fabric-covered fabric covered board.

YOU'LL NEED:

Foam core board for base material, cut to dimensions of your choice

Thin batting, cut to same size as foam core board

Fabric for covering board, cut 4" wider and longer than board.

Ribbon, width of your choice

Decorative upholstery tacks

Glue

HERE'S HOW:

1. Place the batting on top of foam core panel and add dots of glue in a few places to hold it lightly in place.
2. Cut the number of ribbons needed for the criss-cross of ribbons. It is best to trial-cut pieces of string or old ribbon to the sizes needed and place them to see if they will work or if they suit your needs. Then when you are sure you have the measurement and placement correct, you can cut your good pieces of ribbon.
3. Place the fabric panel face-down. Place the foam core panel onto the back of the fabric panel, with batting facing fabric. Pull fabric margins to the backside of foam core board and either glue or tape them to the back of the foam core panel.
4. Place ribbon and attach ends to back of panel by taping in place with masking tape or use glue to attach.
5. Use upholstery tacks where the ribbons cross on the front of the panel.

PICTURE FRAME BULLETIN BOARD

(Not Pictured)

Make a customized bulletin board from a recycled wooden picture frame.

YOU'LL NEED:

Wooden picture frame (one without glass)

Cork sheeting, 1/4" thick, cut to fit the frame

Backing for photo frame, cardboard or thin wood.

Acrylic craft paint

Paint brush

White craft glue

Pliers

Small brads or glazier's points

HERE'S HOW:

1. Remove any nails or brads from the frame with pliers.
2. Paint the frame with the paint color of your choice. Let dry.
3. Glue the cork sheeting to the backing. Let dry.
4. Install the backed cork in the frame. Secure with brads or glazier's points. ❏

CHAPTER 10

Organizing YOUR *Gardening Supplies*

Your garden may consist of a few houseplants in a sunny window, some pots of herbs and flowers on a balcony or in a window box, a small patch of earth along the walk to your front door, or a suburban half-acre with lawn, shrubs, trees, and flowers. How much room you need for tools and supplies is relative to the amount of space you have and the amount of time you spend gardening, of course, but organization will add to your enjoyment.

Pictured opposite page: Here one corner of the kitchen is set aside for gardening supplies. A collection of attractive baskets, buckets, and covered boxes holds gardening supplies in this attractive wall-hung corner cabinet with glass doors and open shelves. The bottom cabinets have a stone slab top that provides a sturdy, easy to maintain surface for potting plants and arranging flowers. Terra cotta pots hold small hand tools, a scrub brush, and a bar of soap for washing up.

This arrangement would also work well in a laundry room that has close access to where the gardening is done. Even a corner of the basement, garage or carport can be made attractive. Kitchen cabinets can be found at salvage stores and painted to look like new. Add some fresh wallpaper or paint to the corner and you have an attractive place for your supplies.

STRATEGY

- Create a home for your gardening supplies. This might be a potting shed, a workbench in your basement, a cabinet on a porch or in a breakfast room or mudroom or hallway, or a wooden box or basket you keep in a closet or on a shelf and bring out when you need it. Having a home means that when you need something you'll know where to look, and you won't buy items you don't need because you have misplaced them.

- Use creative, appealing containers. Terra cotta pots can hold small tools, plant tags, or balls of twine. Wide-mouth glass jars keep seed packets protected and visible. Rustic wooden boxes like old fruit crates can corral bags of potting soil. Baskets are great for lighter weight items like gloves and bags of vermiculite.

- Keep your tools ready to use. Wash and dry hand tools like trowels and cultivators after use to remove soil and keep them free of rust and corrosion. Sharpen the blades of cutting tools to make clean cuts and reduce hand fatigue. Disinfect pots and tools after use to discourage spreading plant diseases.

quick project

GARDEN CARRYALL

A modified fruit crate makes a rustic and useful garden carryall, holding an array of tools and saving trips and time. It's sturdy enough to tote a few reference books and hand tools, and roomy enough to accommodate plant markers, bulbs, garden gloves, and seed packets.

Here's How:

Remove some of the side slats from a wooden fruit crate for easier access. Cut a wooden dowel (this one is a piece of an old mop handle) to fit across the top and through the end pieces of the crate. Drill a hole in each end of the crate near the top and slide in the dowel, then secure with nails or screws from the top. Berry baskets organize and divide the space inside.

Pictured above: A painted bench supports an artful arrangement of potted plants on the edge of a balcony. A metal statue provides a touch of whimsy and adds variety. Space underneath the bench is devoted to storage of clean clay pots and saucers.

CHAPTER 11

Organizing Laundry & Linens

Keeping a family in clean clothes is hard work. Whether your laundry area is a spacious room, a hall closet, or an area set aside in the basement or garage, in a well-organized laundry room the task will go much smoother and faster – and you may even enjoy it.

STRATEGY

- A laundry room should be clean, simple, and totally functional, with good lighting, light colors, and a place for everything.

- Having storage such as cabinets or shelves is essential. You also need a clothes-sorting system, a place to fold clothes, a drying rack (for washables that shouldn't be machine-dried), and a place to hang clothes on hangers. If you iron in your laundry area or near it, you also need space to store an ironing board and iron.

- Organize your supplies and products according to how you use them. Items you use every day should be within easy reach. Rarely used items (e.g., sewing supplies, spot and stain cleaners, dyes) can be placed on higher shelves in labeled boxes that can easily be taken down and stored away quickly.

- When caring for clothes, follow instructions. Adding more detergent than the manufacturer recommends won't get the clothes cleaner, but too much detergent makes thorough rinsing more difficult and busts your household budget. Keep measuring cups on hand. Have the Stain Hotline Number (215-951-2757) handy so you can call to get answers to your stain removal dilemmas.

DIRTY CLOTHES

Get in the habit of bringing dirty clothes daily to the laundry room – this frees up valuable bathroom and bedroom floor space and keeps your rooms fresher. Having all the dirty clothes in one place cuts down on how long it takes you to get a couple of loads of laundry done in a hurry. Since clothes have to be sorted before laundry can begin, have bins ready so family members can sort their laundry when they bring it to the laundry room. Sorting bins make laundry go much faster and more efficiently.

We had a rule in our house once our children were eight or nine years old – "If it's not in the laundry room, it doesn't get washed." You will be surprised how quickly your kids will acquire the habit if their favorite shirt or jeans aren't clean and ready to go when they want them.

CLEAN CLOTHES

Hooks or an expandable rod make a great place to hang clothes for drying or ironing and items fresh out of the dryer. Hooks are also a great place to store laundry baskets when not being used to transport clothes. It keeps them up off the floor and frees up valuable shelf space.

IRONING SUPPLIES

A built-in, fold-down ironing board is the most efficient, but not everyone has a space for one. An ironing board hanger is inexpensive and easy to install. You can even get a hanger that just slips over the top of a door. Look for one that holds both your ironing board and your iron.

STORING LINENS

Most of us have way too many mismatched sheets, old towels, and stained tablecloths that we will never use again. To organize your linens, start by taking them out of the linen closet. As you remove each item, inspect it closely for stains and tears, and check the size. (There's no use keeping twin bed sheets if you no longer have twin beds.) Never keep any linens that are stained or damaged in any way unless you sew and can repair a small hole or tear. If linens are stained but clean, give them to a charity or homeless shelter.

If your closets are small and you need additional space, use your imagination. Old trunks, armoires, chests, and covered boxes make excellent storage spots for linens. You can store quilts, blankets, and sheets inside clean pillowcases or wrap them in acid-free tissue paper. Never store linens in direct sunlight. The edges will fade, and sun rots the fabric.

Sheets:

Color code sheets by size. Use a permanent marker to place a small colored dot on the edges of sheets and matching cases (e.g., red for king size, blue for queen size, green for double). If you have a need for more specific designations (sofa bed sheets, California king), expand your coding system.

It's tough to fold fitted sheets and make them look good. Try this easy tip: keep sheets and pillow cases together and looking orderly on the shelves, slip the folded sheets and one of the cases inside the second pillow case. Tuck under the edge of the case and place on the shelf. Pin on a colored ribbon to code the sheet set's size or designation.

If storage space is at a premium, consider keeping only one extra set of sheets for each bed. You can save lots of time if you get in the habit of removing sheets, laundering them, and putting them right back on the beds. That way, you don't have to fold them, and you save storage space.

Blankets:

Wool blankets need to be stored in a cedar chest or with mothballs to preserve them and protect them from moths.

Quilts:

If you are storing quilts, take them out at least once a year and re-fold them in a different direction to avoid permanent creases and keep them from discoloring. But why keep them hidden? Quilts can be great decorative accessories. To display them, arrange them on a quilt rack, hang them on the wall, or fold them at the foot of the bed.

Bed Linens for Guests:

Purchase or make cloth covered boxes to store extra bed linens for guests. You can stack the boxes in a corner of the room or on top of a cabinet when not being used. They look attractive and make great decorating accessories when color-coordinated with the room. When guests come, simply open the box and make up the bed.

Extra pillows can be slipped into attractive fabric cases, tied with a ribbon, and stacked next to the boxes or on top of them. When you use the sleeping area, remove the pillows from the decorative covers and slip them into regular pillowcases. After your guests leave and you've laundered the sheets, fold them and pack them back into the boxes and slip the pillows into the decorative cases. Re-tie your ribbon and you're done.

Metric Conversion Chart

Inches to Millimeters and Centimeters

Inches	MM	CM	Inches	MM	CM
1/8	3	.3	2	51	5.1
1/4	6	.6	3	76	7.6
3/8	10	1.0	4	102	10.2
1/2	13	1.3	5	127	12.7
5/8	16	1.6	6	152	15.2
3/4	19	1.9	7	178	17.8
7/8	22	2.2	8	203	20.3
1	25	2.5	9	229	22.9
1-1/4	32	3.2	10	254	25.4
1-1/2	38	3.8	11	279	27.9
1-3/4	44	4.4	12	305	30.5

Yards to Meters

Yards	Meters	Yards	Meters
1/8	.11	3	2.74
1/4	.23	4	3.66
3/8	.34	5	4.57
1/2	.46	6	5.49
5/8	.57	7	6.40
3/4	.69	8	7.32
7/8	.80	9	8.23
1	.91	10	9.14
2	1.83		

Index

Continued on page 128

Index